MW01639840

SHUT UP
ABOUT...
YOUR PERFECT KID!™
The Movement of "Imperfection"

Shut Up About…Your Perfect Kid!™

First printing December 2006

ISBN 978-0-9790713-0-0

Shut Up About...
Your Perfect Kid!™

Gina (Terrasi) Gallagher and Patricia (Terrasi) Konjoian

Illustrations by Katie Gallagher and Daniel Terrasi

Testimonials

"*Shut Up About Your Perfect Kid!* has it all. Humor, practical advice and inspiration. Most of all, it is a heartfelt outpouring of love from two mothers with special children who discovered themselves along the way. Read this book and you too will discover yourself."

John Alexandrov, best-selling author of *Your Spiritual Gold Mind, Affirmations of Wealth,* and *The Money Chi*

"*Shut Up About Your Perfect Kid!* provides an articulate, hilarious, and compelling perspective on raising a special child. It should be mandated reading for every parent of a child with special needs and offers parents a welcome respite from the barrage of confusing and sometimes contradictory self-help books usually recommended."

Leslie Spieth, Ph.D., clinical child psychologist

"A book of hilarious, imperfect proportions! You'll laugh, you'll cry, but mostly you'll breathe a deep sigh of relief when you read about all the other parents with wonderfully, extraordinary imperfect kids, just like yours."

Deb DiSandro, founder and president of *www.slightlyoff.com* and author of *Tales of a Slightly Off Supermom: Fighting for Truth, Justice, and Clean Underwear*

"*Shut Up About Your Perfect Kid!* is a delightful compilation of anecdotes from the real lives of sisters Patty and Gina Terrasi who parent their children with unconditional humor and do so with resounding success. Their ability to make the ordinary family experience one of extraordinary poignancy, by honoring the humanity in each of their special children, is a blessing for all parents who struggle with their own family issues of acceptance, expectation, and authority. As an educator and psychotherapist, I am struck by the humility and forthrightness of these authors as they present a long-overdue look at the lives of special families who must contend with a society that emulates perfectionism. Above and beyond the contagious humor within this book is the caveat it contains for all of us: open your eyes to the gifts that each and every one of us bears – young or old, large or small, abled or challenged – you may miss the most brilliant gems in life if you merely scan the surface of human existence."

Sally McCue, LICSW

"Instead of emphasizing the problems they face, *Shut Up About Your Perfect Kid!* celebrates the strengths of children with disabilities and their families.

It illustrates wonderfully the power of humor as a tool for coping with the challenges facing children with disabilities and those who love them.

The combination of warmth and hilarity evident in the stories in this book will help parents of children with disabilities find new ways to maintain a healthy perspective on the joys and pains they face every day. The honesty, openness, and self-deprecating humor of the mothers who wrote this book – and the children who let them write it – provide many valuable and hilarious lessons that will be appreciated by any parent of a child with special needs."

Deirdre Logan, Ph.D.
Psychologist, Medical Coping Clinic and Pain Treatment Service
Children's Hospital Boston
Assistant Professor of Psychology
Harvard Medical School

Let's Get it Started

Over the years, we've repeatedly said that we were going to write a humor book someday. No one believed us – not even our own father. (*"Is this another one of your lame-brained schemes – like the time you two tried to make grape juice by stomping grapes in your kiddie pool?"*)

To be completely honest, we didn't believe it ourselves.

But years ago, a loving family member, the psychic of our family, made a startling prediction. *"You* are *going to write a humor book someday. But it's going to be about raising a child with special needs."*

At the time, we thought she was insane (after all, insanity did run in our family). Who could write a humorous book about such a sensitive subject? How could we make light of our precious children, the kids we struggle so hard to protect every day? And how could we let people in our "perfection-crazed" world know that we had (gasp!) imperfect children?

But over the past year, we encountered other moms and dads of children with a wide range of physical, emotional, learning, and mental disabilities and other "imperfections." We realized that we all possessed a common strength – the ability to laugh in the face of adversity. We also shared some common humorous experiences – from trips to "crazy" counselors to social struggles to sports sagas. And, we were just plain tired of hearing other parents constantly bragging about the accomplishments of their "perfect" children.

From there an idea was born. We would compile humorous, heartwarming, and real stories – ours and those from other parents of "imperfect" children – and put them together in a book that explores the humor and absurdity of raising an "imperfect" child in a perfection-crazed world. A book we've called S*hut Up About Your Perfect Kid!* to finally give "special" parents a chance to talk about *their* children.

When we pitched the idea to moms and dads in our support groups and social circles, they were all for it. *"You have to do this! We're so sick of people bragging about how perfect their kids are and reading depressing books about our children's disabilities. Nobody has a perfect life!"*

Of course, we know that given the sensitivity of the subject matter, some may take offense to this book. We, in no way, want to offend parents of children with special needs. We simply hope to offer them laughter as a healthy coping mechanism, something that has helped our family through some difficult times. And despite the name of our book, we do not intend to attack parents of children without disabilities, but rather tell them why we're proud of *our* kids.

We're privileged to have met so many amazing, caring, and wonderfully imperfect parents, to hear about the accomplishments of their imperfect children, and most importantly, to finally give them a chance to do the talking.

OK, now we'll shut up!

Patty and Gina
"Imperfect" authors/sisters/mothers/daughters/wives/blah/blah/blah

Table of Contents

DEDICATION

To our daughters, Jennifer and Katie, who had the courage to share their "imperfections" with the world. You amaze us every day with your strength and resiliency. You are our inspiration.

And to all other imperfect and special children. We encourage you to continue to think differently – to see color where others see black and white, and possibilities where others see only limits.

One Hot Mama

Protecting her young. It's as natural an instinct for a mother as a Blue Light Special is to a seasoned Kmart shopper. It certainly is for me when it comes to my daughter, Katie, a child with a form of autism. I'm painfully aware of how cruel the world can be to people who are different and am always ready to step in and save her.

Of course, this isn't always a good thing.

"Katie, are you telling me that one of the kids in the neighborhood threw a ball at you? Who was it? I want a name!"

"But Mom, we were playing dodge ball!"

Recently, while watching my niece, Jessica, perform in a school play, I had another opportunity to come to Katie's rescue.

Katie was sitting with her cousins, deeply entrenched in the second scene and holding the program for the play. As she often does with objects she holds, Katie began flapping the program back and forth. Her cousins, used to this behavior and some of Katie's quirkier habits, were completely unfazed.

Unfortunately, three cranky older women sitting in front of Katie weren't as tolerant.

"*Knock it off kid!*" one of them turned around and said.

"*That's annoying!*" said another to a stunned Katie.

"*How rude!*" said the third "golden girl."

Katie's protective older cousin, Jules, was incensed, whispering to me and Katie's father.

"Those mean ladies like yelled at Katie. I just want to like punch their fat heads."

My husband, quite protective when it comes to his daughters, was fuming, whispering to me,

*"Those old bags! I'd like to kick their *&$#!"*

"Calm down! I'll handle those 'blue hairs' at intermission," I said to my husband, who has a full head of gray hair.

When intermission finally arrived, my niece informed me that the ladies were outside smoking cigarettes.

I stormed off to find them with my posse (my sister and all the kids) trailing behind me.

When I spotted one of the women out front, I didn't hold back.

> *"Excuse me, my daughter was sitting behind you inside. You told her that she was rude,"* I said sounding like a teenage boy in puberty.
>
> "*Yes,*" she said staring at me with a blank expression on her face.
>
> "*Well let me tell you Missy! My daughter has a form of autism and has a neurological need to flap that program!*"
>
> *"Oh,"* she said, with a confused look on her face.
>
> *"So before you start* flapping *your gums, you should stop and think that maybe the child might have autism or something they can't help!"*
>
> *"Oh dear,"* she said.
>
> *"Yeah, well we're writing a book for people like you! It's called* "Shut Up About Your Perfect Kid!"
>
> "*Yeah*, Shut Up About Your Perfect Kid!" echoed my sister and co-author behind me.
>
> "*Please accept our apology and sympathy,*" the woman politely responded.
>
> *"Sympathy? I don't need your sympathy! My daughter is a blessing, lady!"*
>
> "*Yeah, a blessing!*" said my sister pointing her finger in the air.

Feeling satisfied (and a bit nauseous), I stormed off with my sister and the kids trailing behind me.

> "*Wow, Gene! I'm so impressed!*" my big sister said in awe.
>
> *"Yeah Auntie, that was like great,"* said my niece Jules. *"One problem though. Like that wasn't one of the ladies!"*

Guide to this Imperfect Book

Stories about Gina (the younger sister) and her daughter, Katie, who has Asperger's syndrome.

Stories about Patty (the nice sister) and her daughter, Jennifer, who has bipolar disorder.

Stories from other "imperfect" parents and their amazing "imperfect" children.

Imperfect Glossary

Definitions of terms and disorders can be found on page 167.

Chapter 1

TO BE "PERFECTLY" HONEST...

"Would you believe my 2-year-old son Dustin is already writing in cursive?"

Perfection. Perfection. Perfection. That's all people care about today.

To be perfectly honest, we're kind of sick of it. In fact, we never even liked playing the *Perfection* board game as kids.

> *"Help me Patty! If I don't fit all these yellow pegs in the right holes, the board is going to explode!"*
>
> *"Mom! How much longer do I have to play this stupid game with her? Little sisters are so annoying!"*

Of course, we didn't realize it when we were kids, but that silly game was really preparation for our lives today as we each struggle to find our right place in a perfection-obsessed world. A world where we have to have a perfect house, be married to the perfect spouse, hold the perfect job, and of course, have the perfect body. It's enough pressure to make *us* want to explode.

As much as we hate to admit it, we, too, have been caught up in this perfection-preoccupation. Not that we're perfect or anything. Heck, we're about as far from perfect as you can get (one peek inside our messy closets pretty much gives it away). We're just terrified of what people in our perfection-crazed world will think of us if we don't at least pretend to care.

It explains why one of us cleans before the house cleaners arrive.

> *"Hurry up Mike! The house cleaners will be here any minute!"* Gina commands while scrubbing the bathroom floor tile with a toothbrush.
>
> *"Gina, this is insane! What the heck are we paying the cleaners for if you do the cleaning?"* he asks, wondering why he didn't stay single.
>
> *"I can't let them see the house like this. They'll think we're sloppy people."*

One of us even keeps the windows closed on 90-degree days.

> *"Why are all the windows closed, Patty? It's stifling in here,"* her husband, Michael, asks as beads of sweat come running down his nose.
>
> *"Oh, yeah, that. I've been yelling at the kids all day. I can't let the neighbors hear. They'll think I'm a bad mother and that I'm damaging our spoiled and disrespectful children's self-esteem."*

The "Perfect" Child

But despite all the perfection we're expected to achieve in our homes, marriages, and jobs, there's no greater pressure than the pressure to achieve perfection with our children.

From the moment our children are born, we have to find ways to make them stand out and be admired by others.

> *"Congratulations on your new baby, Patty! She's beautiful. How did she score on the Apgar?"*
>
> *"Oh Michael and I were very pleased with the results, although they did take off points for her conehead and jaundice."*
>
> *"Oh, that's too bad. Little Mandy had a perfect score. The doctor said he's never seen such a perfect baby!"*

It may be us, but it seems that wherever you go today – the grocery store, the dentist's office, the soccer field, even the business community – you'll find parents eager to rattle off the accomplishments of their children. Parents who will tell just about anyone about their kids, even complete strangers, as Gina learned at a business-networking event.

> *"Nice meeting you, Gina. So what do you do?"*
>
> *"Well, I'm a freelance writer."*
>
> *"Speaking of writing, my 2-year-old son, Dustin, can write his name in cursive already."*
>
> *"That's wonderful. It must really come in handy when he's signing checks."*

Don't get us wrong, we are not saying that this behavior only happens with strangers. Even our own perfection-crazed mother has been known to brag about her 40-something daughters, which is particularly amusing, since she knows better than anyone how vastly imperfect we are.

> *"I told all the seniors in the flu shot line that you girls were writing a book,"* she said, fluffing up Patty's hair.
>
> *"That's great, Mother,"* Gina replied, rolling her eyes and sending a secret signal to her sister.

"They said you guys are so smart. You girls really are! I'm just so proud," she said, picking lint off Gina's jacket.

"Funny, you didn't think that last year when Gina got her third black eye playing basketball."

We are not, in any way, saying that parents shouldn't be proud of their children. Most days (like those rare ones when they actually help with housework), we're quite proud of ours. But as sisters and parents of two daughters with disabilities – bipolar disorder and Asperger's syndrome – we're proud of our kids for a completely different set of reasons. Reasons that sadly don't measure up to most people's high standards of perfection.

Patty, for example, the older sister, is proud of her 13-year-old bipolar daughter, Jennifer, for her courage and maturity.

"Jennifer, are you sure you want to tell your friends that you were in the hospital for depression? They may think differently about you."

"Yeah, Mom, I do. If they're really my friends, they will understand."

And Gina, once a star athlete, is proud of Katie, her 11-year-old Asperger's kid, not for her ability to bounce a ball, but for her ability to bounce back from adversity – time and again.

"Guess what, Mom? I didn't cry today! Not even when those mean girls told me I was too weird to be in their cool club."

Because we have struggled so hard to watch our children overcome adversity, we become frustrated when other parents don't seem to have the same struggles, and often resent the fact that they don't seem to understand ours.

"Katie came home from school really sad. They were playing basketball at gym and the kids were fighting because no one wanted her on their team. Why does everything have to be so hard for her?" confided Gina to a friend.

"Speaking of basketball, did I tell you that Mindy decided to take it up? She was so good; they asked her to move up to the next level. I don't know what it is about her, Gina. She's just a natural at sports."

And though her daughter has a "mental illness" that comes with a different set of challenges, Patty's experienced difficulty relating to others, too.

"Jenn's been struggling so much lately, we were so relieved when we learned

the hospital had a bed available for her."

"Oh, I know how you feel. I was a nervous wreck waiting for Rumer to get into that elite soccer camp. Thank God, we got the last spot!"

But after spending time with these parents and parents of "imperfect" kids like ours, we've been able to put aside our anger and see the humor, irony, and absurdity in the way parents judge their children, and to openly admit just how far we all are from perfection.

We have *all* our children to thank for that, even our "typically developing" kids. And when *these kids* accomplish something big, we try not to brag, especially in front of others.

"Patty that's great that your older daughter Julianne made high honors. You must be so proud."

"Yeah, but I'm even happier that she finally cleaned that messy room of hers."

As parents, our job description calls for *us* to teach our children. Yet day after day, our "imperfect" children are the ones who teach us. They've given us the courage to do what we've been so reluctant to do our entire lives – to be real and embrace imperfection.

And so with tribute to them, we've decided to come out of our messy, disorganized closets to wave our flags of imperfection and openly admit that we sometimes see therapists, experiment with medication for our children, struggle with our loving and over-protective mother, and draw on the silly experiences and expectations from our own childhood.

One thing that will be painfully clear – we will never fit into those perfect places society has made for us. Which is why we've decided to throw away *Perfection* and go for a more interesting game. A game that we think better reflects the complexities of our lives today – *"Twister."*

We invite you to join us and help us show that the true beauty of *all* children is not in how many goals they score or "A's" they earn, but who they are inside.

Sounds like an imperfectly good idea to us.

A "Different" View

One summer, Bitsy, the mother of three "perfect" children, accompanied her mother-in-law, Helen, to California to visit Helen's sister, Ellie.

When they arrived for the visit, Ellie asked Helen about her grandchildren.

"Tell me about your grandkids" she said, turning to her sister.

"I love them all. There's…"

"…my Zachary," interrupted Bitsy. *"He's captain of the soccer team."*

"Wonderful," said Ellie, smiling politely.

"Then there's my Marissa who's in the advanced classes at school," continued Bitsy.

"I see," said Ellie.

"And baby Victoria is already rolling over at two months," Bitsy went on.

"Wonderful," said Ellie. *"How about the* other *children?"* she asked, turning again to Helen.

"Well, there's Melissa's son Kyle. He's…" started Helen.

"…a monster," interrupted Bitsy. *"He's got dyslexia and ADHD. He's completely out of control. I'm telling you if that boy were my child, things would be different.*

Taken aback with Bitsy's insensitivity, the soft-spoken Ellie looked Bitsy straight in the eye, patted her hand, and said, *"No, Bitsy. If Kyle were your child,* you'd *be different."*

Chapter 2

MOURNING THE LOSS OF THE "PERFECT" CHILD AND CURTAINS

"What do you mean you don't want to go shopping? What kind of girl doesn't like shopping for curtains?"

At one time or another, long before we enter the wonderful world of parenthood, we fantasize about what our children will be like. Our mother, affectionately referred to as "June Cleaver," was no exception. Though she would never admit it, "June" probably fantasized about life with a dream daughter: a daughter with striking looks, a flair for fashion, and a burning passion for all things domestic.

It didn't exactly work out that way. Not even on her and "Ward's" second attempt. That's because she ended up with us – two lovable, goofy, domestic buffoons who can't sew a button, yet manage to spend most of their time in stitches.

Of course, when we question our mother if she ever wished she had a "girly girl," her response is always reassuring. *"Are you crazy? I wouldn't trade you girls for the world. Sure, I'd like to see you fix your hair or dust your baseboards every now and again, but I wouldn't have it any other way."*

But the simple fact is, every parent, at one time or another has to adjust his or her expectations for their children. It's not easy; our mother still struggles with it. *"Are you girls sure I can't convince you to go curtain shopping?"*

We wish it were that simple for us with *our* daughters. But when you're a parent of a child with a disability or other imperfection, it can be devastating. It doesn't matter whether it's ADD or ADHD, OCD or PDD, dyslexia or anorexia, the result is the same – you have to mourn the loss of that perfect child and the easy life you had planned for them. Somehow you have to find the strength to leave behind your star athlete, prom king/queen, or class valedictorian and set out on a frightening and unknown path.

So where do you start?

You can go to the bookstore and pick up some self-help books on your child's "imperfection." Not a bad idea, though you may very well have your child pregnant, drug addicted, or living a life of crime by the time they reach age 6.

You could also seek help from mothers of "perfect" children.

> *"Oh I can feel your pain. When little Destiny was not selected as head cheerleader for the pre-school squad, I thought my life was over."*

Or you could squeeze a few minutes in between your busy therapist appointments, battles with your child's school, and trips to the drugstore to read some humorous experiences from other moms and dads who understand how you feel.

You may find your loss is an incredible gain that brings out your inner courage and helps you get to know some pretty special people, including the most special one of all – your precious child.

Not Your Typical Soccer Mom

Gina When our daughter, Katie, who has Asperger's syndrome, was in second grade, we enrolled her in soccer. And while she liked being part of a team, she had very little interest in how the game was actually played – a fact that was somewhat obvious on the field. *"OK Honey, put down the pussywillows! Here comes the ball!"* As a former athlete, I found her lack of interest quite upsetting.

> *"Stop trying to catch butterflies in the soccer net! Pay attention!"*

But nothing upset me more than those looks of pity I kept receiving from the "girly girl" mothers of the "perfect" players. (I knew all about those looks from when I attended aerobics and ended up turning in the opposite direction of the class during *All I Need is a Miracle.*)

There was no question; those moms were feeling pretty cocky watching their children score more than a high school football star. But I was smart enough to realize that they had really accomplished nothing themselves – they were living through their children, something that I did not have to do. And to make them aware of just whom they were pitying, I devised an ingenious plan one Saturday – a defense strategy that had even my husband baffled.

> *"What the hell is that?"* he asked, when I got in the car before a game, wearing my black and orange Maynard Tigers jacket.
>
> *"Oh it's my high school letter jacket, which I earned as a freshman with my three varsity sports. I'll show those 'Cheerleader Moms' that I'm an athlete and don't need to live through my kids."*
>
> *"Gene, you look ridiculous. It's three sizes too small for you. Please take it off. It scares me how much you care what people think!"*

Reluctantly, I took it off.

> *"I guess you're right, Sweetie,"* I said, removing the jacket and revealing my shirt. *"But don't think for one second that I'm taking this fifth grade bowling shirt off. I worked hard to earn all those patches."*

An Outcome Out of Left Field

When Ted, father of 8-year-old Teddy, a boy with ADHD, found out about Little League tryouts in his city, he was eager to tell his son.

"So what do you think Little Man? Do you want to take after your Dear Old Dad and play baseball?" he asked messing Teddy's hair.

"I guess so," shrugged Little Teddy.

On the first day of tryouts, the commissioner of the league announced that they needed coaches.

"Will you coach me, Dad? Will you? Please?" asked Teddy, batting his brown eyes.

"I'm not sure Teddy. That's a big commitment. They have practice twice a week, and Daddy's very busy."

But when he saw the look of disappointment in his son's eyes, he couldn't refuse.

At the first practice, Ted had such a good time, he barely noticed Teddy sleeping in left field.

When they returned home, Ted's wife asked how it went.

"It was great!" said Ted. *"I don't want to be cocky, but I think we're probably gonna take the division."*

"What did you *think, Teddy?"* she asked, frowning at her husband.

"Sorry Dad, but I don't think I want to play baseball. It's kind of boring. Besides it's a big commitment, and I'm really very busy."

Disappointed, but not wanting to push his son, Ted allowed Teddy to leave the team. At the next game, Ted ran into a colleague, the coach of the opposing team.

"So, Ted, which kid is yours?"

Ted pointed beyond the field to the playground where his son and a friend were running toward the swings.

"That one. That's my little guy right there. Wait until you see him swing!"

How Do You Spell Well-Adjusted?

When Joan was a young child, she studied endlessly to get good grades, making her mother ecstatic.

"Guess what Mommy? I got another 100 on my spelling test."

"Oh little Joannie, you've done it again. I'm so proud of you."

But on those rare occasions when she didn't earn a 100, Joan was devastated.

"It's awful! WAAAAAAAAAH!"

"What's wrong, Joannie?" her mother asked.

"I got an 80! My life is ruined!"

Today, Joan's daughter, Kylie, a child with autism, is a spelling whiz with a great memory. With little effort, she brings home 100s week after week, flooding Joan with memories of her spelling glory days.

"You're just like your mother – a fantastic speller. You're probably going to take after me and win the spelling bee. I'm so proud of you."

But one day, Joan's plans were shattered when Kylie brought home a 40.

"Kylie Rose, how could this have happened?"

"I don't know Mom. I guess it was an off day!"

"I don't understand. You get 100s every week."

"I know Mom, but being perfect is so boring!"

By Daniel

Chapter 3

WHY?

"Why our kids? Why us?
Why wasn't there a lifeguard at our family gene pool?"

What makes an ocean wave wave?

Where do babies come from?

Why did you tell that lady at the door with the Bible that you didn't speak English?

Ask any parent today and they will tell you – children like to ask lots and lots of questions. It starts early in their toddler years with queries like *"Juice Momma?"* and continues right through their obnoxious teen years.

"Why do you like always like have to embarrass me?"

"You're not like really like going to wear that like outfit are you?"

We must admit that over the years, we've both become very adept at answering our children's questions with quick-thinking responses like the always effective *"Go ask your father."* Or in this modern era of technology, *"How do I know? Google it!"*

But there is one question for which we have no answer; a question that children with special needs often pose.

Why am I different, Mom?

We wish we knew, but we don't. The fact is, parents of special children have no idea why their children were chosen. We do, however, like to toss around our own guilt-ridden theories.

"It's because I refused the boy in the Resource Room who asked me to the prom. God is punishing me."

"Since I was a kid, I've always eaten too much chocolate."

"It was that glass of wine I had during pregnancy."

"I shouldn't have ordered more epidural."

"Like a fool, I agreed to that immunization."

"It's my husband's fault and my fault for marrying him."

Even our Catholic mother has a theory. *"It's because you girls missed mass in 1984."*

Though the answer escapes us today, we're both confident that our children were chosen for a reason and if (and we do mean if) we make it to the pearly gates of Heaven someday, all will be revealed. In the meantime, we'll keep "Googling" for our answer.

A New Train of Thought on a Difficult Question

Gina

Although God has blessed me with many wonderful gifts (my earlobes are my best feature), he did not bless me with the ability to answer difficult questions. If I don't know the answer to something, it's pretty obvious, which is why I never considered a career in politics or bothered with game shows *("What is. . . I have no idea, Alex?").*

So when Katie came to me for the first time and asked, "*Why am I not like the other kids Mom?*" I was completely caught off guard.

> *"Wwwelll, tttttthat's an excellent question hhhhhoney. Wwwwwwwe'll ask your grandmother tomorrow."*

And that was pretty much how I handled it until one night when I was tucking her in and glanced at her bookshelf.

> "*That's it!* The Little Engine That Could!" I declared, amazed at this brilliant "train" of thought.

I pulled out the book, climbed in bed next to her, and began reading. When I finished, I put the book down on my chest and turned to her.

> *"So you see Honey, you are that little train,"* I said, brushing the hair away from her bright blue eyes.
>
> "*This one?*" she asked, pointing to the cute little blue train.
>
> *"Yes, Honey, that's you."*
>
> *"But that train was so slow,"* she protested.
>
> *"Yes, Honey, but it was the only one that had heart. And I may be biased, but I think you are much cuter than that black train. And let's be honest, that shiny silver one is a bit overdone."*
>
> *"Mom…"*
>
> Steaming ahead with this brilliant analogy, I continued, *"And, as you can*

see there's nothing wrong with you. You got to the same place as everyone else; you just took a different track. Sure, you had to carry a heavy load and make it up that awful hill and then you had to deal with that clown jumping up and down and distracting you…

"OK Mom, I'm that train. Now can I just go to bed? You're making my head hurt!"

Why *Us*?

When we were young children, our parents forced us to share a bedroom, in addition to sharing the same outfits. We lobbied for a bigger house and separate rooms, but they just wouldn't listen. *"Look girls, if Marsha, Jan, and Cindy can share a room, the two of you should be able to."*

It may have been our 7-year-age difference, but sharing definitely wasn't something that came easy for us ("*Mom that little creep took my Magic 8-ball!").* It's ironic that as adults, we've become the best of friends, sharing the same interests, strange sense of humor *("You had a good time at that wake, too? I thought it was me!*"), and most importantly, the experience of raising special children. Yes, we got our tickets at different times and places, yet somehow have ended up on the same wild ride.

GINA'S JOURNEY: Don't Look Now, It's a Curveball

As a childhood tomboy, my favorite sport was baseball. I loved pitching curveballs to my brother. It's funny because that's exactly what life threw me when my first daughter, Katie, was born. I remember the delivery like it was yesterday.

"Congratulations! You have a baby girl!"

"A wwwwhatt?" I asked the doctor, who had a tendency to mumble.

"A baby girl," he said with remarkable clarity.

"There must be some mistake. I'm having a boy. I can't possibly have a girl. I won't know how to do her hair."

But as the months progressed, that beautiful little girl became the love of my life. With her flowing blond hair, bright blue eyes, and long slender legs, I had a suspicion that she wasn't my kid, but I was too caught up in her beauty to look for her biological mother. *("It's not my fault if they mixed up the babies. I'm keeping this one.")*

Her beauty was unmatched only by her easygoing personality. She would spend hours hopping up and down, laughing, and cooing in her Exersaucer (a baby toy not a movie starring Linda Blair). My parents were amazed:

"*You got a great one, Gene. She's such a good kid.*" said my father.

"Yes, most babies are into everything. We can't believe how long she can sit still," added my mother.

She had the cutest little habits of watching TV out of the sides of her eyes and lining up her toys in creative patterns. *("Look Mom, my stuffed animals are on a roller coaster on the stairs.")* When she started using a spoon, I watched in awe as she alternated using her left and right hands. *"She's gonna be a switch hitter,"* I proudly declared to my husband, Mike. *"Maybe this girl thing isn't so bad."*

Years later, when I sent her to preschool, I was eager to receive her first report card to learn just how gifted she was. *"We need to talk,"* the young teacher said, reminding me of my husband when he opens my credit card bill before me.

> *"I know. She's amazing isn't she? What's my 'little prodigy' up to now?"*
>
> *"Well… she has a cutting problem,"* she blurted out.
>
> *"Dear God! I saw that on MTV! I didn't expect her to start with that so early."*
>
> "*No, not that kind of cutting,*" she said, holding up a paper gingerbread man that looked like it had been through a few rounds with Jaws.
>
> "*So big deal, she can't cut,*" I thought to myself. "*So she'll never be a hairdresser or a plastic surgeon.*"
>
> "*It's not just that,*" she said, barely getting the words out. *"She has a poor pencil grip, too."*
>
> *"So she won't grow up and be a bowling scorer. Who cares?"* I rationalized.
>
> *"I'm sorry ma'am, but these are signs of motor difficulties."*
>
> "*Oh well, she gets that from me. My husband's always telling me I'm a horrible driver.*"

Poor motor skills and all, we somehow managed to get through the year with minimal problems. With the blessing of the preschool, we enrolled our daughter in kindergarten.

When I loaded her on the bus that first day, I felt like a mother sending a soldier off to war. Every day, I would rummage through her backpack searching for a shred of information about her "secret life" at school.

Not even a few weeks into the school year, I found it – a letter requesting permission for my baby to be evaluated. Her teacher cited "difficulty following routines, poor social skills," and oh yeah, that "pencil grip problem" again.

I was shocked, but decided to grant permission for the testing. After all, this whole thing was a terrible mistake.

Within a few weeks, I was invited to discuss the results in a Team Meeting. For those unfamiliar with this concept, a Team Meeting is like a celebrity roast without the jokes. You're thrown in a room with five or six teachers who tell you everything that's wrong with your child (the celebrity) and use terminology that you've never heard of, such as "bilateral motor integration" and "WISC," (which I always thought was laundry detergent). My head was spinning during "Katie's roast," when the "Master of Ceremonies" or Team Leader broke through and said, *"Your daughter's social and academic struggles may indicate a learning disability of some sort."*

After that point, I didn't hear anything else.

It would take three independent evaluations and several years for me to truly accept what was wrong with our daughter: a neurological condition known as Asperger's syndrome. We could barely get the funny name off our tongues let alone swallow what it really meant – that she had a form of autism (the dreaded "A" word) that would affect her ability to make friends, get along with others, and perform routine motor tasks. (*"So that explains why she can't tie her shoes! I feel bad for getting frustrated with her!")*

It was devastating to learn that my child was not only not perfect, but was facing a difficult life making friends and performing simple tasks. The reality of it hit me on her 8th birthday, which also happened to be Field Day at her school: a mini-Olympics that would have her class battling it out for all-important bragging rights. Katie was ecstatic.

> *"They're having Field Day on my birthday, Mom. It's going to be so much fun!"*
>
> *"Can I come? Can I, huh?"* I asked, excitedly reminded of my glory days at my elementary school's Field Day when I edged out a girl by a nose (a key benefit of being Italian) in the 440.

"Sure!" she said. *"And can you bring cupcakes? I'd rather eat hot dog rolls, but the kids really like cupcakes."*

When I arrived at the Field Day festivities, my daughter's class was in the middle of a grueling egg and spoon race. Her team was already off to a fast lead.

"Go Katie go!" I yelled, pacing the sidelines with my hands behind my back in cheerleader-like fashion.

"Hi, Mommy!" she said, giving me a smile that could light up a room.

When it came time for her to run with the egg and spoon, I shouted, *"scramble sweetie!"* Then I watched in horror as she dropped the egg, bent over to pick it up and, in a turtle-like pace, drifted over to the other lanes with no idea where she was headed. By the time she reached the pylon on the other side (which was not hers), the opposition had all passed her, setting off her teammates.

"She's making us lose!" shouted our neighbor who was supposed to be her friend.

"Why did we have to get her *on our team?"* said the pretty girl with the "Life is Good" t-shirt.

"She can't do anything right!" said another "friend."

When she reached the finish line, the last one to do so, her teammates walked away shaking their little heads. Then, I watched my sweet little girl sit down on the ground and cry – on her birthday! Not one to just sit back, I shouted, *"It's only a game. I'd like to egg you kids!"* Katie just looked at me and sobbed some more.

Frustrated, I reached for her hand and said, *"Come on, Honey. You don't need this. It's your birthday and we're going home!"*

"No Mom! I'm fine. I want to stay here with the kids," she said getting up.

"But Honey, the kids are being mean!"

"But I want to stay," she said, wiping tears from her eyes.

Not willing to cause her any more disappointment, I gave her a kiss and walked away.

When I got in my car, I sobbed like a baby. And six days later, on my birthday, I was still crying.

That's when it really hit me – my plans for her perfect life would have to be pitched - and somehow I'd have to find the strength to create a new game plan.

PATTY'S JOURNEY: Sobbing right down the middle of Main Street USA

"It's a girl!" announced my doctor. She weighed in at just over 7 lbs, but looked so much smaller.

"Now Jules will have a baby sister to love," I said to my husband.

"Yes but remember you couldn't stand your sister when she was born."

When we brought her home, our friends and family members were amazed, ("*She has such beautiful blue eyes.*"). *I* was amazed, too, especially when she slept through her very first night. Like any neurotic mother of a newborn, I got up every 10 seconds to ensure she was still breathing, thinking, *"She better not be awake all day tomorrow and ruin my plans to watch* Oprah *and* Sally Jesse Raphael." But much to my surprise, she napped for hours and continued sleeping through the night. Still woozy from postpartum euphoria, I was as happy and giddy as a *Price Is Right* contestant.

Yes indeed, life was good.

At about 10 months, she developed separation anxiety. I was actually kind of flattered by it all thinking, *"She likes me! She really likes me!"*

During her preschool years, I started comparing her to her older sister. She was definitely moodier and required more sleep, but I thought that was all it was.

It wasn't until she was 8 that I realized something was terribly wrong.

It actually happened in Disney World, the "Happiest Place on Earth." We were on vacation with all our favorite characters, Mickey, Minnie, Goofy, my Mom, Dad, etc.

We were standing in front of the Magic Kingdom – the hallowed ground where many a Super Bowl MVP had passed. I glanced over at my husband who had never visited this magical place. It was as if I could read his mind, *"Wow! That Minnie has great legs!"*

Just as the parade whizzed by to the tune of *"Remember the Magic,"* Jennifer began sobbing uncontrollably. Soon, people began staring as if to say, *"Hey, bad mother, why don't you shut that kid up?"* I placed my hands over my mouse ears, but it was no use.

And that was just the start. It may have been my Disney daze, but I swear Jennifer "dwarfed" into many personalities during the remainder of the vacation.

There was Saddy – the girl who always cried, like I felt when I learned that *Melrose Place* was canceled.

There was Giddy – the overly happy girl who reminded me of me when I play a round of golf with the same ball.

There was Grouchy – the girl with the pouty face who reminded me of my son when I tell him that Oreo cookies are not a suitable breakfast food.

It was heartbreaking to watch her just plodding away with no real interest in the places we visited or the family members along with us *("What do you mean you don't want to ride Dumbo with your grandmother?").*

When we returned home, I immediately took her to the pediatrician. We began a battery of tests – many of which had acronyms – CAT (which has nothing to do with felines) and EEG (which doesn't refer to anything scrambled, poached, or over easy). Fortunately with my years of medical training as an avid TV viewer of *Marcus Welby, MD* and *ER,* I was a knowledgeable mother.

After all the medical tests were exhausted, we took her to a therapist who suggested Jennifer might have bipolar disorder. My husband and I were baffled. Before we could ask all our questions, a buzzer went off and we were given the, *"I'm sorry, your time's up"* signal.

As we left the office, my husband asked, *"What the heck is bilateral disorder?"*

> *"Bipolar,"* I snapped. *"How should I know? Maybe it's a fear of polar bears!"*
>
> *"That's ridiculous!"* he barked.
>
> *"OK, then maybe it's confusion between the North and South Poles,"* I suggested.
>
> *"Oh great! She got your bad sense of direction."*

When we returned home, I raced to the computer to gather information. It was very frustrating because there was no information available for 8-year olds. There were so many questions to ask; so much I didn't know.

As the days and weeks passed, I would learn a lot more about bipolar disorder, but nothing could prepare me for the painful reality: my baby girl – the one with the sparkling blue eyes who slept through the night – had a serious mental illness. Formerly called manic depression, bipolar is characterized by alternating episodes of mania and depression.

Today, some five years later, I still can't believe it. For me to even utter the words, *"My child has a mental illness"* is still both stunning and extremely painful. Perhaps what is the most frustrating part of this illness is that it is intangible and very difficult to understand. If you're the parent or other family member, you feel utterly helpless, constantly asking yourself, *"What can I do to make her stop being so sad?"*

When I see Jenn running on the soccer field or monopolizing the computer with instant messages to her friends, she seems just like any other kid. But during those manic episodes when she stays up half the night obsessing about a tiny homework project, or those sad periods when she cries for no apparent reason, I realize that the problem really does exist.

Her eyes are still as clear and blue as the day she was born; I just wish her future were as clear.

Why Wasn't There a Lifeguard at Our Family Gene Pool?

Growing up in a large tight-knit Italian family, we shared a lot of strange childhood experiences *("No thanks, Nana, I don't want any more black coffee for breakfast. Besides my preschool bus is almost here.").* One of our most treasured was spending time with our cousins who shared the same interests. Patty and our cousin, Jodi, for example, shared a bond of playing pranks *("Lets put the Sears catalog in Gina's pillowcase. When she puts her head down, she'll bang it.").* And Gina and our cousin Kevin shared a love of flipping baseball cards.

Today our daughters, Jennifer and Katie, share a very different bond as cousins – the bond of living with a disability, though their disabilities play out differently in their lives.

Jennifer, the 13-year-old bipolar child, carries the weight of the world on her shoulders, constantly worrying about the small stuff.

> *"I can't find my permission slip to the field trip!"* she sobs while frantically searching. *"I need it now!"*
>
> *"Calm down, Jenn. When is it due?"*

> *"Not for six weeks, but I have to have it now!"*

Katie, the easygoing, 11-year-old Asperger's kid, just lets the little things roll off her back.

> *"Why do I have to comb my hair, Mom? It's just going to get messy again when I sleep on it tonight!"* or *"Sorry Mom, I forgot to bring my homework home again. Oh well, nobody's perfect."*

Despite the clear differences in their approaches to life, they share a deep bond of love, respect, and mutual admiration, a fact Jennifer proved when she was asked to write an essay in English class about the one person she admired most in this world. She chose Katie because *"Katie always looks on the bright side of things, tries to get better, and makes people laugh."*

Katie looks up to her big cousin, too, though she tends to view the world a little differently. For example, when she found out Jennifer was going to spend a week in a hospital for depression, she said, *"Lucky! She won't have to do homework for a week!"*

Perhaps the greatest strength both these amazing little girls share is their resiliency. Katie probably summed it up best when she said, *"Mom, do you know that song 'I get knocked down, but I get up again?' Well that's me and Jenn's theme song."*

I didn't have the heart to tell her that her mother and aunt share a theme song, too - *Crazy*.

Katie

Chapter 4

WINE TASTINGS, THE CHIPMUNKS, AND OTHER METHODS OF SUPPORT AND THERAPY

"Enough about you doctor, can we talk about my problems now?"

Growing up, our childhood experience with therapy was limited to the group sessions on *The Bob Newhart Show.* We were pretty much convinced that therapy was meant for the likes of Elliot Carlin, the incurable neurotic who had a daily appointment with Dr. Bob.

Today, raising children with issues and being adults with issues of our own, we're proud to say that we've collectively logged more time on the couch than Oprah. In fact, counseling has become such a part of our normal lives that we don't even think about it anymore. (*"Mommy, why do you have the 'feelings doctor's' number on speed dial with the pizza place?"*)

Of course, we realize that therapy doesn't work for everyone. In our experience, there are really three types of people in the world:

1. Those who talk about their problems.
2. Those who bury their problems.
3. Those who talk about their problems and bury them with cheesecake. (Our Italian heritage automatically puts us in this group. There's nothing we like more than discussing what's wrong with our lives over a good cannoli.)

We have a very different view of therapy today – one that Patty sums up well when she says: *"It's the people who aren't in therapy I worry about."*

To us, pretending that everything is fine and perfect seems like too much work. We think it's so much easier and entertaining to just be real. It certainly takes the pressure off, and makes us far more interesting at cocktail parties.

> *"Yes, well my therapist thinks that Katie was just acting out when she threatened to stuff the principal up the school vent."*
>
> *"Personally, I think the magazines at the Salem Psychiatric Hospital are as good as the ones in Lawrence, though the cafeteria food is much better."*

And it makes us both very popular with our friends.

> *"Gina, you always make me feel so much better about* my *life. Thanks!"*
>
> *"So Patty, what do you guys think your mother ate during her pregnancies with you?"*

The fact is, we both have our own way of dealing with the pressures of raising children with issues. Some days, we visit therapists or drown our sorrows in junk food. Other days, we have coffee with understanding friends or watch *Seinfeld* episodes. *("Don't Mom and Dad remind you of the Costanzas the way they argue?")*

The important thing is that we *are* dealing with our issues (or at least trying like heck to).

People who don't have children with special needs sometimes have difficulty understanding this, as one of our dear friends, who is raising two bipolar children, often finds out.

> *"I'm so sick of people asking me, 'How do you do it?'"*
>
> *"I don't think about it. I just do it!"*
>
> *"What am I supposed to do, curl up in a ball and cry everyday? What good would that do my family?"*

We're not saying we never cry or worry. We both have days when we want to cry and escape from our problems. But for us, the best method of therapy is laughter.

> *"I'm telling you Gina. Things are so stressful at home. I got on the highway and had this urge to just keep driving."*
>
> *"ARE YOU INSANE, PATTY? Don't you ever run away from home without picking me up first!"*

GINA'S THERAPY: Non-Stop Talking

Throughout my life, I've employed a very simple strategy for dealing with difficult times – by sharing my troubles and insecurities with anyone who will listen.

> *"I can't believe I didn't get any work this week. My freelance writing business is dying! I just know it!"* I would lament.
>
> *"Ma'am, are you saying you don't want me to Supersize your fries?"*

So when I found out my daughter, Katie, had special needs, I felt the need to share it with the world. After all, I had to shield her from criticism – to let people know that she wasn't rude if she didn't look them in the eye or have fleas because her sensory issues made her constantly itchy. It got to a point where I was telling anyone, *even* those who didn't notice.

> *"Listen, Mr. Cheese, I'm sorry my daughter didn't say thank you or look you in the eye. She really appreciates all your hard work on the birthday party. It's just that she has this disability."*

"Don't worry. None of the kids ever say thank you. It comes with being a rat."

If that wasn't bad enough, I started bringing my worries to my younger daughter's playgroups, interrupting the helpful exchange of information that took place.

"Gymboree is having a sale," a playgroup Mom announced.

"We're going on the Big Red Boat," said another.

"I'm having hamburgers for dinner," said yet another.

"Speaking of burgers, my older daughter has Asperger's."

If I had my way, I would have glued a disclaimer on my daughter's back.

> **WARNING:** This child has been diagnosed with Asperger's syndrome. She is not slow; she just learns differently. If she doesn't look you in the eye, it's because of her Asperger's and not because she is stealing from you. Please be advised that she did not get this from her mother's family. In all likelihood, it came from her father's side. Thank you.

As I told more and more people about my daughter – the mailman, my paperboy, telemarketers, *("Look ma'am, I'm sorry to hear your kid is struggling. Do you want new windows or not?"),* I realized I was not alone. You see, nearly everyone today knows someone who has been touched by autism, bipolar, or some other disability. And very often, you'll find a person who will openly discuss it with you when you least expect it. Someone like my friend, Meghan, a mother of two children with special needs, whom I met while picking my daughter up at school one day. She "had me at hello" when she approached me and asked:

"Hey, do you see that pregnant lady over there?" she said, pointing to an Amazon-like woman whose tattoos made Tommy Lee look clean cut.

"*Oh, I hadn't noticed her,"* I responded with a smile.

"*Well, she just got arrested for smoking crack last week."*

"You don't say," I said, feigning surprise.

"Yeah, and her older kid is an honor student and star athlete," she added. "*It figures. I did everything right, and* my *kids have issues."*

Impressed with her honesty, I asked, "*Would you like to go out for coffee and talk some day?"*

"Sure," she said. *"When would you like to go?"*

"Let's see, I have my therapist on Tuesday, Katie's psychiatrist on Wednesday, occupational therapy on Thursday. So how about Friday at 10 a.m.?"

"Works for me. That will give me plenty of time to go to the pharmacy to pick up prescriptions."

From there, a beautiful friendship blossomed.

PATTY'S THERAPY: Creating a Battle Plan

Before our daughter responded positively to meds, our family was under constant siege. *("Mom, Jenn locked herself in the closet again.")* Survival required careful and strategic planning. Each morning, my husband and I would don our battle fatigues and gather the squadron (i.e., our older daughter, son, and dog) in the "War Room" to review our daily battle plan.

"OK troops, let's meet at 1500 hours to discuss seating assignments for the soccer convoy. Remember, we are trying to avoid casualties."

It seemed that even the most innocent and benign comment would send Jennifer into a dangerous tailspin.

"Gee, Sweetie, your eyes look especially beautiful today. They almost look green."

"T-H-E-Y-'R-E B-L-U-E!!!"

And once she began her downward spiral, it would sometimes take hours for her to recover, something I'm sure our neighbors noticed.

"Is everything all right over there?"

"Sure Mrs. Kravitz. We're just rehearsing a play today. It's called Scream Four (Hours)."

Once, when we were at church, Jennifer crawled under the pew and remained there throughout most of the mass, requiring a quick explanation for the nosy woman sitting next to me.

"Oh, she prays a lot, and her knees are sore from kneeling."

What's most amazing is that throughout her darkest days, Jennifer could control herself the entire six hours she was at school. When she returned home, it was an entirely different story – a fact her brother and sister were quick to pick up on.

> *"Mom, I asked Jennifer if I could borrow a pair of shorts and she growled at me. She's starting to look like Cujo again,"* said my older daughter.

> *"Yeah Mom and she almost bit my head off when I told her we were out of Cheerios. If it's all right with you, I'm gonna dig another foxhole,"* announced my son.

On her most difficult days, I just want to go AWOL. But on some level I know that although we will never truly understand what it's like to walk in Jennifer's boots, our platoon is better equipped to handle life's daily battles.

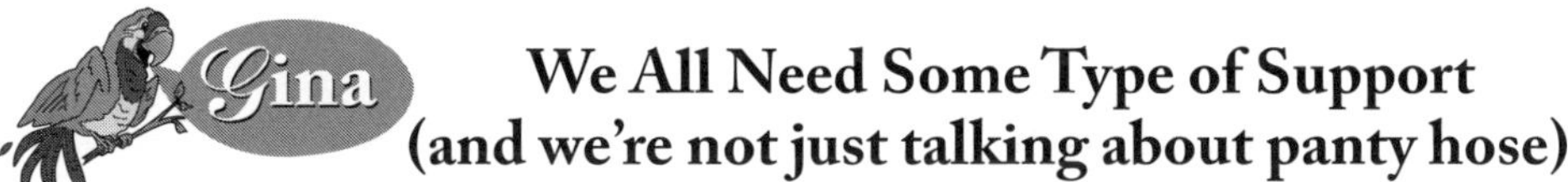

We All Need Some Type of Support (and we're not just talking about panty hose)

With the stress of raising a child with issues in a perfect world, parents must find ways to release their feelings. One of the best methods of support is to talk to others who feel the same way. Support groups offer the ideal solution. But they're not for everyone, as Andrea, a mother of a child who cannot walk or talk pointed out.

> *"I can't go to those things anymore. Women crying all the time. Frankly, it just brings me down."*

In contrast, we have found support groups to be extremely helpful, particularly one that our cousin Jodi, the mother of a 6-year-old child with Pervasive Development Disorder (PDD), invited us to attend.

> *"Patty and Gina, you really should come to our support group. The mothers are all so amazing, helpful, and supportive."*

When we arrived at her house, the group was gathered around the kitchen island, already entrenched in deep and meaningful conversation. *"(Do you like Cool Ranch or Nacho?")*

Jodi, a wonderful hostess, introduced us to the group. *"Say hello to my cousins Patty and Gina"* or *"bipolar and Asperger's,"* and offered us a glass of wine. Eager to overcome our nervousness of meeting new people, and to continue our family's age-old tradition of never refusing alcohol, we graciously accepted. *"Why not? Surely, it will take the edge off."*

One glass led to another, and before we knew it, the entire group (PDD, autism, Asperger's, bipolar, and CP) jelled together, holding up our glasses in unison and declaring to our cousin, *"Hey PDD! More support over here please!"* Within an hour, we were all feeling pretty good about our lives and the state of world affairs in general. And of course, we shared some insightful dialogue.

> *"My daughter is in third grade."*
>
> *"Wow, you have a child? I didn't know that. Patty, did you know she had a child?"*
>
> *"Yes Gina, I'm not entirely certain, but I think that has something to do with the reason we're all here tonight. You know, to talk about our kids."*
>
> *"You have kids, Patty? I didn't know that either."*

Holding Court

Gina

In addition to support from our cousin and compassionate friends like *Ernest and Julio,* we've also been known to find relief through exercise. I, for example, have found women's basketball to be a great way to run out my stress and run through my problems on the court.

> *"So I don't know what to do with my daughter. She's really struggling in math and I'm not certain whether she'll make it through the year,"* I said while dribbling up the court.
>
> *"Are you going to pass the ball or what?"* said one of my team's forwards.
>
> *"I know. Have you ever seen someone talk so much on the court?"* said the other.
>
> *"Yeah, why can't she just trash talk like the other players?"* said the point guard.

Not everyone has accepted this method of coping, most notably my mother, whose favortie sport growing up was meatball.

> *"Why can't your sister quit that sport, Patty! Basketball is so dangerous, and let's face it, she's not getting any younger."*
>
> *"But Ma, she really likes it. She has a lot of friends, and she burns a lot of calories."*

"Why can't she just take up something else that's not so hard on her back – like vacuuming? How do you think I've kept my weight off all these years?"

Driven to Distraction

Unlike Gina, I've chosen a different type of exercise…driving. It may not burn as many calories or be as glamorous as basketball, but if performed carefully, can be less dangerous (I've yet to receive my first shiner). What first began as a little spin around the block soon became a way of life when things got a little too stressful at home.

"There goes Mom again," said my son, Mikey, looking out the window.

"*What? Like she's running away like again?*" said Jules, my oldest, "*That's like the like third time this week!*"

"That reminds me, I need to take her car in for an oil change," said my husband.

It was rather harmless until that fateful day when I was forced to come clean about my coping technique to my pessimistic parents.

"*Patty, what are you doing here at this late hour? And why do you have a suitcase?*"

"Oh well, that's because I ran away!"

"SAINT ANTHONY!" exclaimed my mother. *"I heard about a mother who drove away in her car and found happiness away from her children. That's it! I'm gonna enroll you in the Sacred Heart Auto League."*

"You mean to tell me that with gas nearly $3 a gallon, you can't find a cheaper way to deal with stress?" asked my father.

Music to My Fears

One of the benefits of having elderly parents is the endless education they provide. On one particularly gloomy day, I would learn a strange coping technique from none other than my father-in-law.

It happened during a time when Jennifer was growing increasingly depressed and irritable, putting the whole family on edge, including my mother-in-law, who would receive daily updates from me *("Yeah, Mom, Jenn locked herself in the bathroom again")*. I hadn't really discussed Jenn's struggle with my father-in-law until I had to drop off my car to be repaired, and he came to pick me up.

"Hi, Dad. This is a pleasant surprise," I said, opening the door to his truck.

Immediately, I was struck by blaring music, which made my older daughter's room feel like a monastery.

As I climbed into the cab, I was sure my ears were playing tricks on me. (*"It couldn't be. I must be really stressed. Why would he have* that *on?"*) I asked myself.

But as I listened, I realized I was right. My 76-year-old father-in-law was grooving to none other than Alvin & the Chipmunks. Even more interesting was that Alvin and company weren't singing Christmas tunes; they were belting out Top 40 Beatles tunes *("I Wanna Hold Your Hand")*. To confirm my suspicion, I glanced over to see an empty CD case with pictures of Alvin, Simon, Theodore, and Dave on the cover.

"There's no mistaking this! He's lost his mind!" I thought to myself.

After a few moments of silence, I couldn't help but ask.

"So Dad, what's up with the Chipmunks?"

"Oh, I've just been so upset about Jennifer. I put on the Chipmunks to cheer me up." Then I watched in shock as he crooned in a high-pitch voice, *"I Wanna Hold Your Hand."*

A Sticky Situation

When Art Fry invented Post-It notes, he probably never envisioned the impact they would have on civilized communication. Sure, he knew they would work great for office communication, but I'm sure he never realized how vital they would be in homes. Our home, in particular.

We discovered this during another one of Jennifer's challenging times. With each day, she was having more and more difficulty getting along with people, including her older sister.

"I hate you, Julie!" she screeched at her older sister for borrowing one of her shirts.

"Now Jennifer, please don't say you hate your sister!" I lectured in my calm and soothing mother voice – a voice that would have made Dr. Phil proud.

Julie's response, however, was not as calm, *"I don't know why you like don't just like run away for good, Jennifer!"*

"SHUT UP!" I screamed, returning back to my Jerry Springer Show voice.

"Mom, like that's a bad word," said a shocked Jules.

"Not anymore. She's writing a book about it," said my son fighting back a smile.

I wasn't about to hear it. *"Jules and Mikey get into the car. We're leaving for church!"*

On the way out, I approached Jennifer with what I thought was an outstanding solution. *"Jenn, why don't you try to write down your feelings while we're gone? We'll put your story in the book,"* I said, hoping to calm her down.

Author's Note

During these explosive episodes, it's always best to leave Jennifer by herself so she can calm herself down. Clearly, putting her feelings in writing would be the perfect therapy. At least that's what I thought.

When we returned home an hour later, I realized that Jennifer had taken my advice, though not in the manner I intended. There, wedged inside the storm door, was the latest draft of *Shut Up About Your Perfect Kid!*. Attached to the manuscript was a yellow Post-It note with the words, *"I hate this piece of $%#@!"* scribbled in black marker. Instinctively, I placed a call to my sister and co-author.

"Well, we just got our first negative review of the manuscript," I said.

"WHHHAT? WHO doesn't like our book?" my highly over-sensitive little sister screamed.

As I proceeded to tell her about my fun-filled morning, Jules and Mikey ran up to me.

"*Well, Mom, like I see Jenn was like really busy while we were at like church,*" said Jules as she proceeded to show me a Post-It note which read, *"I hate you."*

"*Yeah, Mom, she definitely did some writing,*" my son said while handing me two more Post-Its with the words *"I hate you!"* scribbled in black marker.

Before I knew it, Jules and Mikey were finding *"I hate you"* Post-Its on the toilet, the refrigerator, the lamps, the dog, and everywhere you could possibly imagine.

Jules exclaimed, *"Whoa! Like hey it's like a scavenger hunt! OK Mikey, I've like got like seven. How many can you find?"*

Realizing that it was a harmless way for Jennifer to get out her anger and that my other children were viewing it all as a game, I went to our local warehouse outlet and bought two cases of Post-Its. Now, our family is communicating better than ever before, including my husband who left me a "*What's for dinner?*" Post-It on the stove yesterday.

Of course, there's always the option of seeing a therapist for support. Today's there's no shortage of excellent counselors and therapists who can help. But like any field, there are good and bad professionals, as Gina and others have discovered.

Back To My Problems, "Dr. MeMe"

Gina

Today, it seems wherever you go, you'll find a person ready to brag about the accomplishments of his or her children. But there is one person I thought would be immune from this. An objective, non-judgmental person who would listen to my anger toward people who just didn't understand me or my daughter.

I found him at one of the lowest points of my life – when Katie started having social difficulties at school and became very sad. *("Mommy, why do all of the kids at school think I'm weird?")*

I was sad, too, something my much older sister was quick to pick up on. "*Look Gene, you're depressing the hell out of me. I think it's time that you get therapy.*"

Tired of spending two-thirds of my family's disposable income on Kleenex, I took my sister's advice and started calling therapists from the Yellow Pages. Most were either too busy or not accepting my husband's insurance. I was just about to give up when I tried one more number.

> *"Sure, I'll take you. You can come right now if you like,"* he said.
>
> *"That's OK doctor, some time this week would be fine,"* I replied, impressed by his responsiveness.

Later that week, I drove up to his home/office. A gray-haired, soft-spoken man, who reminded me of Mr. Rogers, greeted me at the door, putting my fears at ease.

> *"Have a seat,"* he said. *"Sorry if I seem a little tired; I just got back from the White House."*
>
> *"You did?"* I asked, impressed with the man I carefully selected, and eagerly anticipating when he would change into his boat sneakers and cardigan.
>
> *"Yes, I take photographs as a hobby. The President was so impressed by one that I did of the American flag that he invited me to the White House."*
>
> *"Wonderful,"* I politely replied, waiting for him to bring up my favorite subject – me.
>
> *"Yes, it was all very amazing. I'm still quite shocked by the whole thing,"* he said.
>
> *"Yeah, well that's great, but I have this daughter…"*
>
> *"In fact, people are constantly calling me trying to buy my photographs. I'm building a second studio you know…"*
>
> *"Yeah, yeah, that's all good. Now about my daughter…"* I interrupted, hearing my precious minutes of therapy ticking away.
>
> *"Yes, your daughter. Tell me what's wrong with her."*

Finally, the response I was looking for.

> *"Well, she's struggling and I'm having a really hard time accepting…"*
>
> *"I have a daughter,"* he blurted out. *"She's amazing."*
>
> *"That's great, but…"*

"In fact, she graduated at the top of her class. On Parent's Night they told me she was one of the brightest students to attend her school."

"Terrific. You must be proud," I said, wondering what new, innovative form of therapy he was using. Surely, it was only a matter of time till he turned things back to me.

"She's on a full scholarship you know."

I listened to him drone on and on, and then before I knew it, my time was up. He sold me a copy of *The Assertiveness Handbook,* and I was out the door. When I returned home, I recounted this twisted tale to my husband, who always sees the good in people.

"Well Gene, maybe he was caught up in the excitement of the White House. I think you should give him another chance."

Like a fool, I took his advice and went back for my next appointment. This time, "Dr. MeMe," greeted me in the driveway.

"I thought we'd meet in my studio."

"Wonderful," I replied, silently cursing my husband.

He ushered me inside where I saw his beautiful photographs. I complimented him on his work and sat down on the couch, eager to share my deepest, innermost thoughts, fears, and insecurities.

I told him that I was worried about my daughter's academic future and whether she would ever go to college.

"Speaking of college," he interrupted. *"I teach at the local state college. During the graduation ceremony, a student gave a speech about the one person who influenced her life the most. I was shocked when she said it was me."*

"Wow," I said, silently searching for an object to kill myself with.

"Do you want to see the video? I have it on tape."

"NO! That's not necessary, doctor. Don't go to any trouble on my behalf. After all, my time is almost up."

"No it's no trouble; it will only take a minute. Let's see where did I put it? Oh yes, I think it's in the office in my house."

While I watched "Fred Rogers" fumble into the main house, I experienced a moment of remarkable clarity. *"Hey, my life's not so bad. He's a psychologist and he's crazy as a loon. My problems are nothing compared to his!"*

By golly, his innovative therapy had actually worked.

Reverse Psychology

One winter day, Jose´ and Maria were on their way to a world-renowned hospital to see a psychologist about their young daughter's anxiety disorder.

On the way, they encountered a fierce snowstorm, making for a treacherous drive and a very anxious Maria. *"Step on it Jose´!!!"*

They arrived at the appointment a mere ten minutes late and received a "frosty" greeting from the doctor.

> *"You are vedy, vedy, late,"* said the doctor.
>
> *"Wwwwwwwwe're so sssssorry ddddddoctor,"* chattered Maria, taking a moment to wipe an icicle off Jose's nose.
>
> *"We left in plenty of time, but the road conditions were horrible and Jose´ insisted on stopping at every red light!"*
>
> *"Nebertheless, you are vedy, vedy late,"* scolded the doctor, scribbling furiously in her notebook.

Frustrated, Jose´ shot Maria an angry look – the same look she received the week before when she announced that her mother was coming for an extended visit.

> *"Whut brings you here?"* asked the doctor.
>
> *"My little girl is having panic attacks, and difficulty making friends at school, and I'm so worried about her,"* cried Maria reaching for a Kleenex.
>
> *"Whut I see here is vedy, vedy, bad padenteeng,"* said the doctor, scribbling some more. *"Whut else?"*

"Well, she's been getting into fights on the bus and her grades are slipping," said Jose´, taking Maria's hand in his.

"Again, vedy, vedy bad padenteeg," she said, scribbling yet again.

For the remainder of the appointment, Jose´ and Maria underwent intense questioning that would make even Barbara Walters squirm. Somehow they found the strength to hold it together. The car ride home was an entirely different story as they tried to make sense of the painful visit. *"It's your fault Maria!" "No, it's your fault Jose´!"* They finally reached an agreement when Jose´ said, *"You're right Maria. I don't think we should stop at red lights."*

A week later, an anxious Jose and his daughter arrived to the next "scheduled appointment." When the receptionist saw them, she was startled, telling Jose´, *"I'm sorry Mr. Rodriguez, you don't have an appointment today."*

In Johnnie Cochran-like form, Jose´ produced the card confirming the appointment. *"If the appointment card fits, you must admit."*

Confused, the receptionist paged the doctor while Jose´ and his daughter waited. Ninety minutes later, the doctor arrived sporting Roseanne Roseanna Danna-like hair and a wrinkled coat. Even worse, she was "flying lower" than a discounted airline.

"My God!" Jose´ thought to himself. *"She just came from a quickie!"*

Eager to get back at the doctor, who made his life miserable and nearly destroyed his marriage, Jose´ said, *"You're late!"*

Fumbling for her fly, the doctor replied, *"I'm sorry. My doog was seek."*

Not missing his opportunity, Jose´ scolded, *"This is vedy, vedy bad doctoring"* and flew out the door with his daughter.

A Few Rounds of Therapy

When Victoria, a mother of a bipolar pre-teen, was worried about her son's aggression problem, she decided to try a new therapist. The therapist was eager to jump in the ring and go at the problem head on.

"Wonderful, Mrs. Augustino, you and Nathan meet me at my office next Tuesday at 11 a.m. and bring a pair of boxing gloves. We'll work that aggression right out of him."

Startled by this hard hitting form of therapy, but eager to find relief, she agreed and brought her son and the boxing gloves to the next appointment.

A well-dressed man in a suit and tie greeted them and ushered Nathan into his office. With time to kill, Victoria perused the magazines in the waiting room. She had just about fallen into REM sleep when she was awakened by a loud bell.

The door to the office flew open and Victoria was greeted by the disheveled therapist. "*We're all set here,*" he uttered breathlessly, removing his crooked glasses from his forehead, tucking his shirt back in, and loosening the tie that was wrapped around his neck.

"How did he do?" a concerned Victoria asked.

"He did great. What an uppercut!"

At that moment, Victoria's son, *"Sugar Ray,"* burst out of the room, jabbing the air and dancing around his mother *"You want a piece of me Mom? Huh? Huh?"*

"I CAN'T TAKE HIM HOME LIKE THIS! Victoria screamed. *"HE'S ALL WOUND UP! YOU MADE HIM WORSE!"*

"*Don't worry Mrs. Augustino. Just bring the boxing gloves next week, and we'll work that aggression right out of him,*" he said taking out his appointment book. *"So what do you think? Should we schedule the next round of therapy now?"*

And then there are therapists who provide good advice.

And They Called It Puppy Love

When Katie reached third grade, her social struggles really began to worsen. *("The kids think I'm creepy because I flap my hands.")*

Watching her come home and cry after school was more than I could handle. So I took a drastic step – I took her to a child psychologist – something that surprised my mother ("*SAINT ANTHONY! My granddaughter is not crazy!*").

When I told the psychologist about Katie's eroding self confidence and difficulty making friends at school, he made a startling suggestion.

> *"Get her a puppy! Kids love puppies. It will help her make friends."*
>
> *"A wwwwhat?"* I stuttered. You see, I was not a "pet person." My childhood pet experience was limited to Peppy, an adorable white poodle with a built-in Radio Shack transistor radio.

There were so many things I loved about that dog. His fluffy white fur. Little button nose. And unique ability to give me the latest weather updates and sports scores. I don't ever remember a moment when he wasn't there to listen to my problems and see me through my childhood tribulations. (*"Oh, Peppy! Mom wants me to wear a dress to the wedding! It's just awful!")*

But the years were hard on Peppy. His nose fell off from my constant kisses and eventually, he lost all broadcast capabilities altogether. Even worse, he began to shed his toothpick-like stuffing all over our house.

> My sister, resentful of my relationship with Peppy, constantly complained about him. "*Do I have to share a room with that disgusting rag? All she does is kiss it. It's so gross!*"
>
> My mother stood by me, constantly performing surgery on Peppy to repair his wounds. *"There Honey, I sewed his head back on. Do me a favor and try not to hug him so hard next time."*
>
> But one day, she had had enough. *"Honey, I think it's Peppy's time. He's old and dirty and his stuffing got in the shag rug and clogged my Electrolux. I don't understand why; I thought I closed him up real good last time."*

With my heart as broken as Peppy's AM/FM tuner, I handed him over to her, completely devastated. Too devastated to even realize that my sister had sabotaged Peppy by breaking up toothpicks and scattering them over the shag rug.

On our last day together, I gave Peppy one final decapitating bear hug. I retired to my room and promised never to love another dog and have my heart broken again.

That was the plan. But now the psychologist was foiling it for me. Even my husband, who had pets during his entire childhood, was jumping on this puppy parade. *"Come on Gene. Let's get me, I mean her one!"*

To determine the best dog for us, we went to an Internet search site and typed in our qualifications. I entered my preferences – low maintenance, non-smelling, non-shedding, self-cleaning, durable, knowledgeable, and obedient. I hit the search button and almost instantly, a picture of a transistor dog like Peppy popped up. It was a Bichon Frise, a cute fluffy white dog ideal for children. My husband wasn't so sure. *"He's cute and all, but won't I look like a sissy walking this fluffy white dog around?"*

We decided to visit a breeder and view one in person. When we laid eyes on a scruffy little one that looked like Albert Einstein, we instantly fell in love. For a moment, I even felt like Peppy had come back to me.

"We'll take him!" we told the breeder.

When we brought him home, Katie was ecstatic. *"Oh, he's so cute! I can't wait to show the neighborhood kids. Thanks, Mom and Dad! This is the best day of my life! I will never forget it!"*

We watched her take her puppy outside with her little sister in tow. Just as the doctor predicted, the neighborhood kids came running over, hugging and wrestling with our puppy.

The smile on our daughter's face was worth a 1,000 puppies.

"We did good, Sweetie," my husband said, putting his arm around me.

"Yeah, we did. I just wish those kids wouldn't hug him so hard. They're going to knock the toothpicks right out of him."

Two Sides to Every Story

Gina

Over the years, Katie has had numerous therapist appointments with both her psychologist and psychiatrist. And like a lot of people who meet Katie, they've become quite taken with her. *(Mrs. Gallagher, she really is very funny!)* But sadly, Katie hasn't reciprocated their feelings. (*"Why do I have to go see them? It's so boring. All we do is sit around and talk about feelings, feelings, feelings!"*)

On one particular day, she put up quite a fight about going to the psychiatrist.

> *"Oh no! No way am I going there today!"*

But fortunately, my strong parenting skills helped me manage that one.

> *"If you go, I'll buy you a pizza!"*
>
> *"Make it an iPod Mom and I'm there!"*

When we arrived at the psychiatrist's office, Katie took her usual spot on the big blue couch. Within moments, she began squirming around, eventually landing in her normal headstand position against the couch. I used this opportunity to share my concerns with the doctor.

> *"Doctor, I met this parent of an Asperger's child who said his child hears voices. Is that something that I can expect from Katie?"* I worriedly asked.
>
> *"Well with neurological conditions like Asperger's, it is possible. But let's ask her,"* she said, turning her head upside down to talk to Katie.
>
> *"Katie, do you hear any voices?"*

Katie dismounted from her headstand and said, *"Oh yeah. I hear two all the time."*

> *"Really?"* asked the doctor. *"Tell me about these voices."*
>
> *"Yes! Please tell!"* I said, straightening up in my chair.
>
> *"Well, one is on the right side of my head and the other is on my left,"* she said, looking out of the sides of her eyes, as she so often does.
>
> *"What do they look like?"* the doctor asked.
>
> *"Yeah Katie. What do they look like?"* I asked, fighting back panic.

"Well, one looks like me and has a pitchfork and the other looks like me and has a halo. And they both tell me what to do. Sometimes the one with the pitchfork wins and that's when I do bad things. So, Mom, when I do bad things, it's not my fault."

"And what kind of bad things does she tell you to do?" the doctor asked.

"Wwwell…she sort of…kinda of...like she…," she said stalling and continuing to look out of the sides of her eyes.

"Katie, are you making this up?" the doctor asked.

"Yeah all right. You caught me. I am *making it up. But I do hear a voice in my head that tells me what to do. That's the truth I swear."*

"And who is it?" we ask in unison.

"Oh, it's just me."

A Pregnant Pause

Humor and absurdity are not just limited to the therapist's office. We've known parents who've experienced moments of humor at the most stressful times and the most stressful locations. Parents like Annie, mother of Emily, a 10-year-old girl born with a mitochondrial defect, who is confined to a wheelchair, unable to speak, and kept under 24-hour care.

When Emily began suffering seizures, Annie was instructed to check her into the hospital for testing.

When they arrived, they were escorted directly to a room and Emily was carried into her hospital bed. Annie was sitting by her bedside when a nurse arrived with a shiny new computer on wheels designed to "simplify the admission process."

"*OK, Ms. Haynes, I'm here to ask you some questions,*" the nurse said, rolling the computer over to Annie on the bed.

"*Yeah, yeah, I know,*" said Annie who frequented emergency rooms with her daughter and was used to having more questions thrown at her than Alex Trebek.

"Are you ready?"

"Bring it on," said Annie prepared for the usual ridiculous set of questions she is posed every time she checks her daughter into the hospital.

"OK, what's your daughter's name?"

"Emily."

"How old is she?"

"*She's 10.*"

"What's your daughter's sex?"

"*Oh, like most daughters, she's a girl.*"

"Is your daughter ill?"

"Yeah," said Annie, watching her daughter twitch like a Mexican jumping bean.

After a series of endless questions the nurse said, *"OK, I just have one last question and we're done."*

"Sure, go ahead," said Annie, confident that they had all the ridiculous questions behind them.

"Is there a chance your daughter is pregnant?"

Blaa

Chapter 5

ANYTHING YOUR KID CAN DO, MINE CAN DO DIFFERENTLY

"My kid's a track star."
"Yeah, but we bet ours can bolt faster than yours."

We've all seen and heard from them. They're in our cities and towns. On the soccer fields. At swimming lessons. Behind the bulletproof glass at ballet class. They're the mothers and fathers of the perfect kids. You know them – the ones who drone on and on about how smart, athletic, gifted, and talented their children are. Blah, blah, blah.

And despite the fact that we might live in the same neighborhood, attend the same PTO meetings, or even drive the same minivan, we are worlds apart from them – with different goals and different ideas of success. In fact, at times, the differences are so great that it really feels like an Us vs. Them world.

For example:

Them:
"Little Montana loves soccer. She's chasing the U-6 soccer record."

Us:
"Jane loves soccer, too. It gives her a chance to chase butterflies."

Them:
"I was ecstatic to learn that Logan is at the head of the class."

Us:
"I was ecstatic to learn that John went *to class."*

Them:
"Princess is involved in many activities. She has ballet on Monday, soccer on Tuesday, and theatre on Wednesday.

Us:
"Susie's involved, too. She has OT on Monday, counseling on Tuesday, and tutoring on Wednesday. And did I mention the new social skills workshop she's starting on Friday?"

Them:
"Chelsea just loves hamburgers with pickles. She loves to eat."

Us:
"Katie just loves hamburgers without the hamburger. She barely *eats."*

"Sticking" it to Them for a Change

And if it's not bad enough that we have to listen to them, we have to read the bumper stickers on their minivans and SUVs. That's OK, because we've come up with our own in response:

Theirs:
My honor student loves me.

Ours:
My bipolar kid loves me and hates me.™

Theirs:
My child was student of the month at St. John's.

Ours:
My child was patient of the month at St. Elizabeth's.™

Theirs:
I'm spending my soccer star's inheritance.

Ours:
I'm spending my kid's inheritance on co-pays.™

Theirs:
This car drove up Mt. Washington.

Ours:
Some days, this car wants to drive off Mt. Washington.™

No Newsletter is Good News

Even worse than their bumper stickers are the newsletters that often accompany their holiday cards – those painful greetings that go on and on about every accomplishment their child has made since the first trimester. A typical "perfect" newsletter might go something like this:

*To our friends, family,
neighbors, and colleagues:*

Holiday greetings to you and yours. Now it's time to hear about ours. Little Dakota was the first child in Gymboree to graduate to Pull Ups. He's following in the footsteps of his big sis, Felicity, who is the top tapper in her dance class. My pregnancy is progressing beautifully though I am feeling a little heavy (I now weigh a healthy 105 - a size 4 dress!). The ultrasound showed we're having another girl. We've named her Jasmine and she's already reading in utero! Dakota, Sr. loves his new career in rocket science and between watching the kids grow and saving the whales, he and I are keeping very busy.

For periodic updates on all our lives, including our prized poodle, Muffy, visit our website at www.PerfectJonesFamily.com."

These newsletters are by far the greatest annoyance of the holiday season. We think "imperfect" newsletters would be much more popular and appreciated by readers.

To our dear friends, family,
and psychiatric professionals:

It's been a banner year! We began by getting a new minivan complete with a navigation system. It's been a lifesaver! We have the routes to all the nearest hospitals and pharmacies pre-programmed. With the time we've saved from printing out directions, I'm now able to spend some time knitting. I'm just starting out but I made little Rebecca a new sock to chew on. (This has really helped her stop chewing the couch.) John is doing well. He landed a third job hauling trash, which helps cover all our psychiatric co-pays.

We are so proud of Little Bobby. During his last incarceration, he received the prison's coveted Inmate of the Month award for his good behavior. And John and I were so impressed by the license plate he made for us for Christmas.

Rebecca is just terrific, too. Her soccer coach has noticed that she's kicking harder than ever (though it's still at the other players). And the other night, she actually sat down and did her homework.

It's been a bittersweet year, as Felix, our cat, is no longer with us. One of the kids left the door open, and he never came back. John says he's never seen a cat run so fast.

Well, that's all the news we have to report for now. Best wishes for a happy, healthy, and hospitalization-free holiday season.

The Dysfunction Family

A Few "Choice Words" for Bragging Parents

We really don't mean to be so hard on parents who brag endlessly about their children (OK, we do). It's just hard to listen to how good *their* kid is on the baseball field when *yours* would rather catch real flies. Or how great *their* kid is doing in school when *yours* won't go to school.

But we're not foolish enough to believe that these people are actually living perfect lives. We think it's all a matter of word choice. Some of us parents of imperfect children are guilty of creative phrasing of our own.

Like Meghan, the mother of two special needs children, who tells people that she lives in a "gated community."

Translation: She has to keep gates up all over her house to protect her children from falls.

Or us when we let it slip at cocktail parties that our money is "tied up in pharmaceuticals."

Translation: We have more meds in our medicine cabinet than a hypochondriac.

Or our pal, Susie, who tells people she has a "driver" take her daughter to school.

Translation: Her kid gets picked up in a city-funded minivan.

Then there's single mother, Andrea, who tells people she's "seeing a handsome doctor."

Translation: She's in therapy.

Artists. Inventors. Star Athletes. Our Children Are Different and in Good Company.

Over the years, we've both been suckers for the latest trends. We *were,* after all, among the first children in our neighborhood to get Jordache designer jeans. And we did jump on that Twist-A-Braid craze before all others.

Today, we're part of another growing trend – having a child with special needs. Think about it. With the explosive growth in learning disabilities and mental disorders, it's chic to have a kid with "issues" today. Of course, any time you jump on a trend, you can sometimes get criticized by others (we know this from our

Dorothy Hammill haircut experiment as kids). And when you have a child with special needs, you and your child have to be prepared for all kinds of criticism.

> *"What kind of bad mother lets her kids throw a tantrum in the produce aisle?"*
>
> *"What a foul mouth! That Tourette kid needs a spanking!"*
>
> *"There, there, Little Aurora. If Kira hurt your feelings, it's only because she's slow. Don't pay any attention to her!"*
>
> *"An IEP (Individualized Education Plan) is just a poor excuse for bad behavior. I would never put my kid on one."*
>
> *"Who orders a pizza without cheese?"*
>
> *"Give me your bipolar kid for a week and I'll whip him into shape."*
>
> *"Doesn't it bother you that your child is costing taxpayers so much money?"*
>
> *"How can you put your daughter on medication – aren't you worried about the long-term effects?"*

Those of us who live day in and out with our children know better. We know that if they "flap" a butter knife in a restaurant, it's not because they are threatening the waitress, but because they have a neurological need for stimulation. If they appear "slow," it's because they think differently. We like to think of our children as Macintosh computers operating in a world full of PCs; they get the same answers but process things differently.

In fact, many people would be shocked to discover the famous people who have diagnoses of depression, bipolar, and learning disabilities. The National Alliance for the Mentally Ill (NAMI), a nationally recognized advocacy group, has identified the following famous people with mental disorders:

Depression

Abraham Lincoln (President of the United States) – I'd put my money on him any day.

Charles Dickens (Author) – Now you know what the Dickens is wrong with him.

Ernest Hemingway (Author)

Mike Wallace (Television Host)

Sir Isaac Newton (Scientist) – Of course, that apple to the head didn't help matters.

By Golly, Look Who's Bipolar

Winston Churchill (Prime Minster of England)

Ludwig van Beethoven (Composer) – He'd be rolling over if he knew the criticism our kids get each day.

Vincent Van Gogh (Painter) – As if losing an ear wasn't bad enough.

Patty Duke (Actress) – No wonder she's so believable in those sad Lifetime movies.

Learning Disabilities

According to schwablearning.org, the following famous folks have tackled life with learning disabilities.

Whoopi Goldberg (Actress) – She's so popular, they named a cushion after her.

Cher (Singer) – Where would Sonny have been without her?

Jay Leno (Talk Show Host/Comedian)

Charles Schwab (Financial Guru) – "Talk to Chuck?"

Greg Louganis (Olympic diver) – In his day, he made quite a splash.

Terry Bradshaw (Football star/actor)

Tony Bennett (singer) – No wonder he left his heart in San Francisco.

Bruce Jenner (Olympian)

Patrick Dempsey (Actor) - You may even call him "Dr. McDayDreamy"

Henry Winkler (Actor/Director) – "Heeeeeey!"

Vince Vaughn (Actor)

Harry Belafonte (Singer)

Lindsay Wagner (Actress) – Yes, even bionic women can have disabilities.

Plus, these celebs are also known to have learning disabilities.

Tom Cruise (Actor) – He's got Dyslexia and made a career reading lines.

Robin Williams (Actor)

Walt Disney (Creator) – Some say he was in his own little world.

And if that still doesn't impress you, check out the following famous people who were thought to have serious learning disabllities. What a difference they've made in our lives.

George Washington (President) – Might explain why he chopped down that cherry tree.

Thomas Jefferson (President)

Alexander Graham Bell (Inventor of the Telephone)

Albert Einstein (The smartest man in the world) – It's neat to throw your kid's name in the same sentence with his. (*"Yes, Katie and Albert Einstein think similarly."*)

Thomas Edison (Inventor) – Imagine if he did not have the ability to think differently. The world would be dark.

She's BAAAAAAAACK

Gina When Katie was 7, she asked to join ballet. It was particularly difficult for me whose ballet experience was limited to the ballerina who performed in my childhood jewelry box (the comfortable home of my baseball cards). But her argument was so convincing, I just had to give in.

"P-l-e-e-e-e-a-s-e, Mommy. P-l-e-e-e-e-e-e-a-s-e."

"All right, I give up. But you can get any mother/daughter dance routines out of your head!"

In silent protest *("Maybe I'll try and bribe her out of doing this")*, I enrolled her and somehow managed to muddle through the endless Saturday morning sessions, which spanned three long seasons. "*You know Mike,*" I said to my husband. "*I could conceive and give birth to a baby and this ballet season would still be going on.*"

At first, Katie seemed to enjoy it, but during the final "trimester," her interest began to wane and mine began to perk up, especially after I paid for her costume for the recital. It was a big investment, one I was determined to get a healthy return on.

My daughter, of course, had a different plan.

> *"I don't want to be in the recital! Ballet is too hard,"* she protested, when I asked her to try on her costume the first time.
>
> *"Are you crazy?"* I fired back. *"Do you have any idea how much I spent for that costume? You're not only going to wear it to the recital; you're going to wear it for Halloween and possibly your junior prom."*
>
> *"But Mom, I don't want to do ballet anymore, and the costume is too itchy."*

I just didn't want to hear it. Quitting was not an option – something I knew from my high school sporting days when I found out I had to wear a skirt in field hockey and asked my father if I could quit. *"A Terrasi never quits,"* he told me.

I sure wasn't about to. So when we arrived at the recital, I yanked my daughter out of the car, receiving strange looks from the other mothers.

> *"I don't want to do it!"* my daughter protested.
>
> "*Oh you're doing it! A Terrasi never quits,*" I fired back.
>
> *"Noooo!"* she screamed. *"Besides, I'm a Gallagher and we do quit!"*
>
> Panicked, I started negotiating with her, *"Please Honey, I'll buy you anything. How about a pony?"*
>
> At that moment, my childhood friend, there with her daughter, came to my rescue.
>
> *"Gina, get lost!"* she said.
>
> *"Excuse me?"* I asked, perplexed.
>
> *"Go away. As long as you're here, she won't go on. Let me take her backstage."*

Reluctantly, I went to sit down with the 89 other family members on hand for the event.

"She's not gonna to do it!" I sobbed to my mother.

"SAINT ANTHONY!" exclaimed my mother. *"But her hair looks so beautiful, and you already paid for the costume."*

"The way you kids waste money today," said my father, shaking his head.

"Gina, you don't give her enough credit," said my sister, Katie's Godmother, and one of her biggest fans.

Feeling helpless and disappointed, I sat back and prepared to watch the recital, which would not include my daughter. As I watched all the performers, I wondered why my daughter wasn't like them and why things were always so difficult.

After what seemed like days, I heard the familiar song and watched as members of my daughter's troupe filed onto the stage. I was shocked to find my daughter bringing up the back. Excited, I notified my family members. *"Mom! Dad! Everyone! Wake up! Katie's on the stage!"*

She kept right up with the girls, mirroring the steps she had learned over all those grueling weeks. I was instantly flooded with fond memories of my jewelry box ballerina with one minor difference – my daughter never faced the audience. During the entire performance, she faced the back wall, never once looking out at us.

It didn't matter; I was ecstatic.

"Honey, you did great. I'm so proud of you," I said running up to her after the show and giving her a hug. *"The back of your head looked beautiful."*

"Thanks Mom, but do I have to do this again? Ballet is kind of boring and I was really nervous.

"OK Honey, it will be hard, but Mommy will try and get by without it," I said, crossing my fingers behind my back.

"And can I take off this stupid itchy costume now?"

"You bet Honey," I said, hugging her. *"You don't have to wear it any more – at least not until your junior prom."*

❧ A Shining Example of Toughness ❧

We always knew our bipolar daughter, Jennifer, had a fighting spirit. We just didn't realize how strong it was until we went to pick her up after a 10-day psychiatric hospitalization.

As my husband and I nervously walked the corridor to Jennifer's room, a teenaged girl jumped out in front of us, blocking our path.

"*Wait! I have to tell you something! Your like daughter like saved my life!*" she blurted out.

"*Oh I know,*" I said. *"Jennifer also gives out great fashion advice. Once she saved me from embarrassing myself with this out-of-style jacket."*

"NO! I like mean it! She like really saved my life!"

My husband and I just stared blankly at each other while she explained.

"Well, like this really like scary kid, Zachary, was like really mad at me and was just about to like punch me in the face when Jenn like stepped like right in front of his fist."

"That's great. Thanks for telling us," my husband said, nudging me along toward Jennifer's room.

When the young girl was out of sight, I stopped my husband and whispered, *"She must be delusional. I've read about that psychosis."*

But when we stepped into Jennifer's room and saw our little "Rocky" with her first shiner, we realized *we* were the delusional ones. Our daughter was a bigger fighter than we realized.

A Chip Off the Old Rock

At one time or another, most parents think their children don't listen to them. But when you have a child with ADD, who constantly needs to be reminded to do things over and over again, it becomes a way of life.

One day, Fernando was surprised to discover how well his son, Tony, a bright child with ADD, was listening to him. They were driving in the car to meet Fernando's wife and daughter at the pediatrician's office. Fernando was in a good mood, singing and rapping on the dashboard to his favorite rock 'n roll songs.

Suddenly, his moment of peace was interrupted, *"DAD! HELP DAD!"*

"*What is it Tony?*" Fernando screamed, turning down the radio to hear what had his son in such a panic.

"*I've got a rock in my nose!!!*"

"A what?" he yelled back.

"A rock up my nose!" shouted Tony.

"Just hold on while I pull over," said Fernando.

Fernando pulled over and jumped in the backseat to look up Tony's nose.

"Oh Jesus Christ!" he yelled. But when he remembered where they were headed, he settled down. *"Well that's OK, we'll just have the doctor take it out when we get there."*

Pleased with his emergency preparedness, he got behind the wheel and resumed singing only to be interrupted by young Tony again, this time with a question.

"Hey, Dad, who is this Jesus Christ anyway?"

"Well, it's kind of a long story and you'll get to learn more about it when you get older and go to religion class. But, to make a long story short, Jesus was the Son of God."

"Oh, I know him. That's the guy you always talk about – God Dammit!"

A Clear Head on A Cloudy Day

One day, Clara, a 5-year-old girl with PDD, decided to work on an art project. She tore up small pieces of white paper and glued them onto a white sheet of paper.

When she finished her creation, she excitedly ran up to her father.

> *"Look at what I made, Daddy!"* she said putting it under his nose.
>
> *"Wow Honey,"* said her father. *"I see clouds. And there's the sky. And oh look, over here are little birds flying in the air."*
>
> She grabbed the paper from his hand and said, *"No, Daddy, that's not right. I just ripped up pieces of paper and glued them."*

Ode Dear

One evening, while being tucked into bed, Sara, a 6-year-old with PDD, posed an important question to her mother, Barbara.

> *"Mommy, can I get a pet to play with?"*
>
> *"Well, Honey, a pet is a big responsibility. Now isn't the right time. But you do have all these stuffed animals to play with,"* she said, pointing to the shelves of stuffed monkeys, bears, and turtles that filled Sara's room.
>
> *"OK, Mommy. Goodnight."*

The next morning, as Barbara was ascending the stairs to Sara's room, she was startled to hear Sara talking to someone.

> *"Odie, would you like another biscuit?"* asked Sara.
>
> *"Ruff, ruff,"* said Sara speaking for Odie.

Curious, Barbara listened outside Sara's room. When she finally entered the room, Sara said, *"Hi Mom. I was just having tea with my new friend, Odie. Would you like to meet and pet him?"*

"You know I would Sara. Anyone who is a friend to you is a friend to me."

"Odie, this is my mom. Mom, this is Odie," announced a proud Sara.

Barbara turned in amazement to discover that Sara's new pet was not at all imaginary, or even a stuffed animal. No sir, Odie was none other than an Odor Eater.

Chapter 6

FROM VITABALLS TO RITALIN IN 60 SECONDS

"I think this prescription will really help with the distraction, organization, and forgetfulness problems."

"Wonderful doctor, I'll start taking it immediately."

"It's not for you; it's for your child."

There's no shortage of controversial subjects in America today. There's the burning Roe vs. Wade dispute, the age-old Republican vs. Democrat battle, and of course, the always divisive paper vs. plastic debate. But there's another controversial topic drawing battle lines all over the country and the world – medication. It seems everyone has a strong opinion about it, including our mother, a lifetime subscriber to *Tragedy* magazine, *"Ya know, I just read that Ritalin causes cancer in sea urchins."*

And if the great William Shakespeare were around today, he'd probably be involved in the debate, too – *"To medicate or not to medicate; that is the question."*

As passive women who hate choosing sides (we both drive our cars straight through forks in the road), we are not in any way advocating medication. We can tell you, however, that both our children *are on* medication. What started off with harmless Vitaballs and Flintstones Chewables has escalated into more powerful drugs to help our children function on a daily basis. *("Mom, I didn't fall asleep in math today. That medicine really works.")*

But the decision to medicate was not any easy one for us, nor is it for any parent. One only has to listen to the side effects to figure that out: Headache. Nausea. Sleeplessness. Frequent urination. Weight gain. And that's just from the guilt for us parents alone, not to mention the side effects for the child.

The fact is, for parents, the subject of medication can generate more outrage and guilt than a *Lifetime Television for Women* movie marathon. We've met parents who feel guilty for *putting their kids on medication* and parents who feel guilty for *not putting their kids on medication*. Heck, we've even met parents who feel guilty for *taking their kids'* medication. (*"That Ritalin really helped. You should have seen me organize those closets."*)

Take Two Pills and Play Dollhouse with Me

Gina

When we were little, my friends and I were fascinated with the *Guinness Book of World Records*, always trying to come up with creative ways to see our names in print. *"Do you think 100 pieces of Bazooka will be enough?"* I drooled to my girlfriend, nearly choking on the blob of gum in my mouth.

I didn't know it then, but I was *already* a Guinness record holder for achieving an amazing accomplishment: having the most fights with my older sister. You name it, we fought over it from the time we were little, right up until she was in college.

> *"You've been drinking, Patty. I'm telling Mom. How else can you explain that dent you put in the bathroom wall with your head?"*

My sister wasn't much better. *"Mom! How much longer do I have to share a room with that little creep?"*

Sadly, my two daughters, Katie and Emily, have carried on the tradition of fighting over everything. Emily, my friendly and impatient 7-year old often becomes frustrated with Katie's laid-back, daydreamy attitude toward life. And Katie, who treasures time to herself, gets tired of Emily constantly following her and bossing her around.

"Katie! Get out of La-La land! Your bus is gonna come!"

"*Mom! Emily's acting like you again!*"

Their inability to get along has never deterred Emily from trying to convince Katie to play with her.

"*Katie will you play dollhouse with me?*"

"*Go away, Emmy! I'm on Katie time!*"

One day, Emily approached me with a brilliant solution.

"Mommy, can you give Katie some medicine so she'll play dollhouse with me?"

Ritalin Me This

When Sandy learned her teenage daughter had ADD, she began a quest for knowledge, obsessively combing the Internet and self-help books to find out more about this strange disorder. As she uncovered the symptoms, she grew more and more concerned. *"Lack of attention span... daydreaming.... forgetfulness... dear God that's me! I have ADD!"*

Having made that scientific breakthrough, she was ready to begin her treatment program. So that morning, along with her Special K and orange juice, she swallowed one of her daughter's Ritalin. She and her daughter did, after all, have a very close mother/daughter relationship, sharing clothes, jewelry, and now stimulants.

"I just want to see what it's like," she rationalized.

When she arrived at her company a half-hour later, she found a mountain of work at her desk. Within 10 minutes, she had plowed through it all and made coffee for the entire first floor. She was vacuuming her keyboard when her boss stopped by and said, *"Sandy, I just want to tell you what a great job you're doing."*

She didn't continue the Ritalin, as her company had just implemented a new employee drug testing policy. But rumor has it that her actions that day got her serious consideration for Employee of the Month.

Love Can't Keep it Together

When Betsy and her husband, Mitchell, first learned that their middle child had bipolar disorder, they went to see a psychiatrist.

"*We've found that some medications can really control bipolar,*" the psychiatrist said.

"*That's great, doctor, but we're from a loving family,*" Mitchell said, gazing into his wife's brown eyes. "*Love will see us through.*"

"*Yes doctor,*" agreed Betsy, rubbing Mitchell's back. "*Surely, our strong family ties can overcome this thing you call bipolar disorder without medication.*"

"*It's your choice. But here's my card if you change your mind.*"

"*Oh we're firm on this,*" they said, holding hands as they walked out of the doctor's office.

Upon their arrival home, they were flagged down by their older daughter, Geri Anne.

"*Mom! Dad! You better come quick!*" she yelled, grabbing their hands and taking them to the backyard where they found their bipolar child, Julie, chasing their youngest child, Mitchell Jr., with a horseshoe for "taking the last blueberry Toaster Strudel."

"*I'm going to ring your neck!*" Julie screamed. "*How could you do that to me?*"

"*BETSY! WHAT DO WE DO?*" screamed Mitchell in full panic.

"*The Captain and Tenille were wrong! Love can't keep us together. I'm calling the doctor right now. We're getting her on medication – tonight!*"

Katie
Shut up
about your perfect
kid

Chapter 7

FOOD FOR THOUGHT

"Yes my daughter would like a Happy Meal. Please hold the meal and she'll be happy."

Food and drink. They're the centerpieces of Italian culture. As young impressionable girls raised in a 100 percent Italian household, we quickly learned the importance of food and drink to our people. Food and drink were, after all, love. To refuse either from our relatives would mean we were, in essence, refusing to be loved.

> *"Gina, your grandmother just called. She was very upset and wanted to know why you didn't finish your high ball."*

> *"But Mommy, I'm only 6."*

You see in an Italian family, all of life's milestones, setbacks, and challenges are dealt with in the same manner – with food and drink.

We eat and drink when we're sad.

> *"Oh Gina, I'm so sorry the Red Sox lost to the Yankees. How about a bowl of spumoni to cheer you up?"*

We eat when we're happy.

> *"Patty, that's so wonderful that you lost five pounds. How about we celebrate with manicotti and wine?"*

We feed a cold and feed a fever.

> *"My poor Bobby has the stomach flu. Let me make you chicken soup with meatballs."*

Knowing this, you can imagine how difficult it was for Gina and our parents to accept Katie's eating habits. Like a lot of children on the autism spectrum, Katie eats only a handful of foods – pizza, bread, cereal, and yogurt. And when you attempt to give her anything "off the menu," she freaks.

> *"What did you put on my plate, Mom? I 'm gonna hurl!"* she screamed running to the bathroom.

> *"Katie, it's a French fry!"*

Her dislike of French fries has baffled Gina and prevented her from sharing her favorite fast food experience with her daughter.

> *"Mommy's going to McDonald's. What do you want Sweetie?"*

"Great. I'll take a Happy Meal without the meal!"

Birthdays and holidays are a challenge, too.

"Are you ready to blow out the candles on your birthday cake?"

"OK, but don't think for one second that I'm' eating that disgusting thing."

Katie doesn't even like candy, something Gina learned the hard way.

"Mike, I just don't understand why these pants don't fit me anymore."

"I don't know, could it be because, maybe, you ate all of Katie's Halloween candy yourself?"

Sometimes we worry that Katie is missing out on an important part of her Italian heritage, but when we see her long thin thighs and fret about our meaty ones, we think she might be on to something.

If only we weren't so loved.

A Slice of the Pie

Gina

Other than anxiety *("SAINT ANTHONY Katie! Your report is due tomorrow!),* my mother and I have very little in common. Her childhood nickname was Golden Hands, for her unique ability to make something out of nothing. Mine was Butter Fingers for my uncanny ability to make a mess out of anything.

She's also a killer cook, while I kill with my cooking. You see, for an Italian girl, I'm not exactly good in the kitchen, something my husband likes to remind me about.

"Gina, can you get me a snack in the kitchen?"

"What's that?"

"Oh, it's the room with the stove and refrigerator – you know the big metal thing that holds the bon bons.

"Oh, yeah! I know it now!"

So when it comes to feeding my family, I have to be resourceful. This is especially important when you have a child who eats just a handful of foods.

Thankfully, one of those foods is pizza – a relatively healthy, inexpensive, and most importantly, deliverable food.

Katie would eat pizza every day and be happy *("Mom, when I grow up, I'm going to have pizza for Thanksgiving").* This has worked out well for my family and for the local pizza franchise in our city, which greatly benefits from my lack of culinary talents and Katie's lack of interest in all other foods.

> *"Mrs. Gallagher, I'd like you to meet your new account rep,"* the head of our franchise told me when I opened the door one day to accept my delivery.
>
> *"Oh hello, what happened to Romeo, my last delivery man? The kids and I had fun with him. 'Oh Romeo, Romeo, wherefore art our pizza?'"*
>
> *"Oh, he bought a second home with the money he made off your account and retired."*

The frequent delivery visits to my home have also caused a stir in my neighborhood. Even my neighborhood pal, Juli, is looking at me differently.

> *"So what's going on with you and the pizza guy? Come on, you can tell me. I won't tell Mike."*

It hasn't taken long for other pizza establishments in our city to try to get our business and gain a "piece of the pie." But Katie has stood firm with her brand loyalty despite our attempts to get her to change.

> *"Come on, Honey. Can Mommy order the pizza from somewhere else? It's kind of embarrassing!"*
>
> *"You're telling me, Gene,"* my husband added. *"They told me that we've already called 289 times this year. And it's only February! So what do you say, Katie? Can we get the pizza somewhere else?"*
>
> *"No! I want* our *pizza place! Besides they named a pizza after us – The Gallagheroni."*

Toying Around with Lunch

Gina One of the side effects of Katie's medication is that it lessens her appetite, particularly during lunch time. This posed a problem when it came to packing her lunch every day. Each morning, I would send a nutritious lunch that represented all the four main food groups, and each afternoon it would return untouched. My husband and I were sickened by the amount of food she was wasting. *("Do you know how many children in Africa would die for that Fruit Roll Up?")*

Our daughter, however, was unfazed.

"Mom, hurry! Pack my lunch. The bus is coming!"

"But Katie, you don't eat lunch!"

"So!"

This was in stark contrast to her little sister, Emily, who would eat every morsel in her lunchbox.

"Emmy, where's your ice pack? I don't see it here in your lunchbox."

"Uh oh, I think I ate it."

Katie's wastefulness at lunch got to a point where it was causing a rift between my husband, Michael, and me.

"This is such a waste, Gene. I say we don't pack a lunch."

"Are you crazy? The school will call DSS on us! We have to make it look good. Now hand me the wheat germ."

We were baffled about what to do, until my husband came home from work one day with a Toys 'R Us bag and a brilliant solution.

"Look what I got, Gene," he said, holding up the bag.

"I thought I got you off that Playstation addiction," I said, disgusted.

"No no, it's not that," he corrected, removing a plastic piece of chicken and sunny side up egg from the bag. *"It's plastic food for Katie's lunch. We'll put it in her lunchbox, and her teachers will never know."*

"So simple yet, so brilliant," I beamed, remembering why I married this sharp man.

"So what do you want for dinner?" I asked, while searching through the bag and pulling out a few items.

"Spaghetti with meatballs or lamb chops?"

Chew On This

Sometimes "special" children are not just fascinating for what they don't eat; they're equally interesting for what they do eat. Many times, it doesn't involve food, but common household objects. Jane, the mother of Carla, a 9-year-old autistic child, witnessed this one morning while getting ready for work.

"Where the heck are all my nylons?"

"I know," said her younger daughter, Annie. *"Carla's been eating them."*

"What do you mean she's been eating them?" Jane asked.

"She puts them in her mouth and then hides them in the couch cushions."

Curious, Jane went down to the couch only to discover a pile of soggy stockings underneath all the cushions.

"That's disgusting! Now I'll have to wear sandals!" she said.

Later that evening, Jane joined her friend, Mindy, also the mother of an autistic child, for a quick drink.

"Wow! I've had such a hard week!" said Mindy.

"Yeah, me too," said Jane.

"Connor has been so difficult this week."

"So has Carla. She's been doing some strange things."

"Like what?"

"Well, it's kind of weird. I'm embarrassed to tell you."

"What is it? Just tell me."

"Well, she kind of....sort of... has been chewing on all my nylons."

"Yeah, I know what you mean? Connor's been chewing on the backs of our new oak kitchen chairs."

"Really?" said Jane, already feeling much better about her daughter's nylon nibbling.

"Yeah, we even purchased furniture protection. But the furniture store sent us a letter saying that they wouldn't cover it because it was obvious that it was from animal damage. I don't what kind of animal could do that type of a damage – maybe a 3-foot beaver?"

By Daniel

Chapter 8

FIELD OF DAYDREAMING

**"Mommy why do we have to follow the ball?
It's more fun following a bee."**

When we were children, sports were designed to develop coordination, team building, and most importantly, self-esteem. Today, you can pretty much pitch that idea away like a Roger Clemens fastball. Children of all ages are now taking to the baseball diamonds, soccer fields, and hockey rinks with a single purpose – to win at all costs.

We figured that out when we attended a youth basketball game recently.

> *"Foul him!"* a mother shouted.
>
> *"Yes, get him!"* shouted another.
>
> *"So what if he's on our team. Just don't let him shoot!"*

That's nothing compared to the *behavior* of some parents. One needn't go any further than the newspaper to learn about that:

> *"Baseball Dad clubs opposing pitcher."*
>
> *"Hockey Mom sticks it to coach for not giving child playing time."*

The competitiveness of sports today has made it difficult for a lot of children. And that's especially true for those with special needs. But we question whether our special children, the kids who seem distracted or confused on the field, simply prefer not to get caught up in the insanity of it all. Maybe they would just rather "kick back," enjoy their time in the sun, and follow a butterfly.

Sounds like a winning idea to us.

Score One for a Little Underdog

Gina

To help my daughter, Katie, with her soccer skills, I was constantly practicing with her in the back yard. And though she shined against her four-year-old sister and neighborhood cats (who preferred to play with yarn), it was a completely different story when it came time take to the field.

Generally, if the ball was on one side of the field, she was on the other, usually in a different time zone altogether. But she wasn't the type to just stand around. No sir; she made the most of her playing time either by following butterflies or gathering a bouquet of dandelions for me.

To inspire her to get into the game, I developed a complex rewards system early in the season.

> *"OK Honey, every time you touch the ball, Mommy will pay you a quarter."*
>
> *"Awesome! Let's play!"*

Midway into the season, she had accrued 25 cents, which she got on a technicality. She was sitting on the sidelines eating orange slices when someone kicked the ball into her.

> *"Mom,"* she called, holding out her hand. "*You never said I had to be* on *the field."*

During the final game of the season, when I watched her take the field in her clean uniform, I realized that she probably would never touch the ball, let alone score a goal. I also realized that it was still pretty cool being the mom of the Cleanest Player on the Field.

But when the half ended and she came to me with tears in her eyes, I realized that *she* wanted more.

> *"What's wrong, baby?"* I asked.
>
> *"Everyone scored a goal but me. Kids say I'm not very good."*

Heartbroken, I got down to her level and gave a speech that would have made Knute Rockne proud – a speech that closed with powerful words that amazed even me. *"And if you score a goal, I'll buy you that beauty parlor set you've always wanted."*

When I watched her take her position on the field and ignore a beautiful butterfly on the way, I knew something was different. *"Look Mike! She's on the same side of the field as the ball,"* I yelled to my husband. Then, she ran to the ball and started kicking it down the field. One, two, three times.

> *"MIKE, SHE'S KICKING THE BALL! LOOK AT HER GO! SHE'S UP TO 75 CENTS!"*
>
> *"GINA! SHE'S GOING THE WRONG WAY!"*

That's when it hit me. I was married to one of those sports-crazed dads I often saw on the news.

Moments later, she was standing in front of the opponent's net when the ball came her way. In a Hokey-Pokey like motion, she put her right foot out. The ball bounced off her foot and started rolling toward the left goalpost. I jumped out of my seat and in Carlton Fisk-like fashion, began waving my hands to the right toward the goal.

The ball bounced off the post and trickled in. The mothers on the field erupted.

Then my little soccer star came rushing toward me with open arms. It was a Kodak moment – and one of the greatest of my entire life.

After the game, one of the mothers approached me.

> *"Gina, your daughter just scored her first goal. What are you going to do now?"*
>
> I picked up my daughter and proudly declared, *"I'm going to buy a beauty parlor!"*

Screamin' for Ice Cream

When he found out his Little League team had made it to the baseball finals, Aaron, an 8-year old with ADHD, was ecstatic. *"My team's going to be World Champions!"* he proudly declared to anyone who would listen.

When the big game finally arrived, Aaron took the field with pride.

The game was a tight one, scoreless until the bottom of the fifth inning, when Little Aaron stepped up to the plate with the bases loaded. He planted one foot in the batter's box and was just about to bring in the other, when he was interrupted by the sound of the theme from *The Sting* blaring.

Instinctively, he dropped his bat and went running to this mother and father.

> *"Mom! Dad! The ice cream man! Can I get a Two-Ball Screwball! Please!"*

A "Street-Wise" Dad

When Steve and Lynn watched their 8-year-old son, Tom, with ADD play hockey in the driveway, they were very impressed.

"*Wow! What a slapshot!*" said Steve. *"Let's enroll him in street hockey."*

"Are you sure it wouldn't be too hard for him? Hockey may be kind of confusing," said Tom's protective mother.

"He'll be fine," said Steve.

In the first practice, young Tom shined. But during the first game, he had difficulty determining which direction to go. Making matters worse was the fact that his team switched sides during the change of every period.

"*STEVE! HE'S GOING THE WRONG WAY!*" screamed Lynn sitting with Steve and the other parents in the stands. *"DO SOMETHING!"*

Instinctively, Steve jumped out of the stands and yelled, *"Tom, follow Dad!"*

Steve then got to the edge of the rink and began running back and forth in the direction of the game.

It was a brilliant plan that worked well as Tom scored two goals (none of which were for the other team).

At the end of the game, Lynn was ecstatic, running up to her son. *"Oh, Tommy, you did great!"*

"You did!" affirmed the parents in the stands next to Lynn.

"He did, too!" said one father, pointing to Steve who was walking breathlessly toward them.

"Yeah," said another. *"What a hustler! He ran hard the entire game!"*

A Kid on the Ball

At times when our children seem to be lost in space or in their own world, they surprise us with just how on the ball they are. Such was the case with Mary, a 10-year-old diagnosed with Non-Verbal Learning Disability. One day, Mary was sitting in the stands during her mother's championship soccer game when a loud husband of one of the players began yelling out inappropriate comments at the opposing team and banging on the stands – all while holding his preschool daughter in his lap.

At the end of the game, Mary took a seat next to her mother on the bench and said,

"Mom, do you see that guy over there?"

"Yes, Honey, what about him?"

"He's got some serious *issues."*

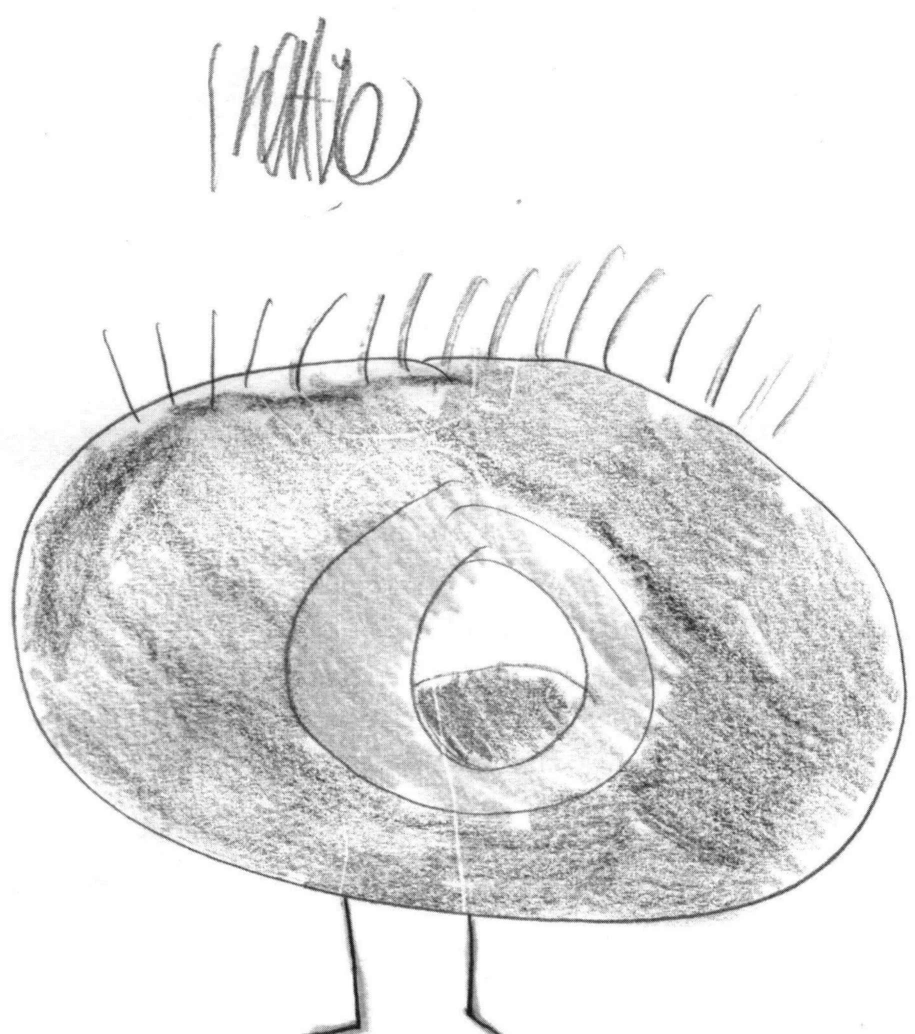

Chapter 9

WOMEN ARE FROM VENUS; MEN ARE FROM THE PLANET OF THE APES CHANNEL

"You can remember the name of Beaver Cleaver's first grade teacher, but you can't remember to put your son on the bus?"

Let's face it. Marriage is not all wine and roses (or in our families, beer and dandelions). Today, married couples are faced with more pressures than a tropical storm – from the increased cost of living to increased cable channels in today's "digital divide" (*"You're watching the Planet of the Apes channel again?"*). And if you're raising a child with a disability, the stress is even greater *("Do you know how much money you spent on co-pays, Patty? I'm going to have to put you on a therapy budget!").* It's not surprising to learn that so many parents raising kids with disabilities end up divorced.

The fact is, men and women are very different. And that's painfully obvious when it comes to raising children. Gina realized that difference the first night she brought Katie home from the hospital.

> "*Wow! She's amazing! She slept through the night already! This parenting thing is a piece of cake,*" her well-rested husband, Mike, exclaimed the next morning.
>
> "*No pal! You slept through the night! We've been up 6 times,*" a weary Gina snapped.

Yes, even today, it's pretty amazing that despite everything that goes on with our children – social struggles, anxiety, depressions – our husbands still always manage to sleep soundly. Patty's husband is no exception.

> *"Michael, I can't sleep a wink. I can't believe Jennifer has a mental illness and is in the hospital. Our baby girl, all alone, so far from home. Doesn't it seem surreal?"*
>
> *"Zzzzzzzzzzzzzzz."*

Of course, we're not, in any way, saying that our method of staying up all night and worrying senseless is better, especially when we wake up with more bags than Wal-Mart shoppers and our husbands look as fresh as daisies. It's just a simple fact that women tend to worry more, and men have the ability not to dwell on things. *"So what if I gained a few pounds? I'll take it off someday. Now be a sweetie and grab me the hot fudge."*

Upgrading Memory

Though women worry more than men do, we also remember more. When it comes to our children, we mothers have the storage capacity of 100-gigabyte hard drives. Our husbands, on the other hand, could use a memory upgrade.

"What pills am I giving our daughter again?"

"The same ones we've given her every night for the past 5 years."

"Oh, right, and which daughter is it again?"

That's not so bad until you realize what they do remember.

"Do you know I can recite every Super Bowl MVP since Super Bowl I?"

"Ask me any of the vital statistics of any Sports Illustrated *swimsuit model."*

"Diane and Elaine Klimaszewski. Those are the names of the Coors Light twins."

An "Incomplete" Assignment for Dad

When Cheryl, a successful work-at-home executive and part-time student, was heading to class for the night, she gave her husband, Tony, a list of instructions.

"Take out the trash, walk the dog, and please help Anthony (their child with ADHD), complete his homework.

Eager to calm his frazzled wife, Tony assured her, *"Cheryl, I've got it all under control. Now get out of here!"*

When she left, Tony was eager to "get to work."

"Anthony, do you have any homework?" he asked his son.

"Nope," said Anthony confidently.

"YES!" yelled Tony, pumping his fist in the air and crossing off homework on the list Cheryl had left.

Not long after, Cheryl called to check in, asking in a Judge Judy-like tone,

"Did Anthony do his homework?"

"He didn't have any," replied Tony.

"Really?" Cheryl said, raising her eyebrows in suspicion.

The next morning, while Cheryl was getting Anthony ready for school, a frightening thought occurred to her as she prepared to open his backpack. *"This is like a bad accident. I know I shouldn't look, but I have to."*

When she saw what was inside, she was furious. Not only did Anthony NOT DO his homework, he also neglected to study for a quiz.

Seething, she called her "better half" who was in the car enjoying a quiet drive to work.

"DID YOU KNOW ANTHONY HAD HOMEWORK? YOU DIDN'T TELL ME HE HAD HOMEWORK!"

"I asked him and he said he didn't," said Tony.

"AND YOU BELIEVED HIM?"

"Calm down, Cheryl."

"I'm not gonna to calm down. If I'm melting down, you're going to melt with me."

"Cheryl? Cheryl? I can't hear you. Must be a bad cell. Why don't we talk about this later? And by the way, I'm working late, so don't wait up."

A Depressing Family History

When Kathy and Steve received the diagnosis of bipolar disorder for their daughter, they sought a second opinion from another doctor. When they arrived for their appointment, a young intern greeted them.

"I'll need to take a family history of mental illness from each of you. It only takes a few minutes," the intern said, taking out a clipboard.

"Steve, why don't you go first?" Kathy said, removing a thick pad of paper from her pocketbook.

"Well OK, I'm not sure, but I think my 4th cousin once went to a

psychologist for trauma related to a car accident. But that's all I can come up with."

"Good," the intern said. *"Now it's your turn, Kathy."*

"OK, I have a few things," she said, opening up the pad of paper, which made *War and Peace* look like light reading.

"My mother is a germaphobe."

"My grandmother suffered postpartum depression when she had my mother."

My cousin on my mother's side has a serious gambling addiction. He bet all his children on 'red' once."

"And my mother's brother's son is a cross dresser."

"Then there's my great uncle. He thinks he's General Patton."

Two hours later the intern said, *"I think we have enough Kathy."*

At that moment, a shell-shocked Steve turned to Kathy and mouthed, "*Omigod Kathy, your family! I never knew!*"

Kathy, who is very close to her extended family, shot back, ("*Oh yeah! Well my family may have depression, but your family* causes *depression.")*

Then she turned to the intern and said, *"So, are you ready to hear about my father's side now?"*

Kathie

Chapter 10

SIBLING RIVALRY:
THE OTHER SIDE OF DONNY AND MARIE

"Come on Mom! Pleeeeeeeeeease write about me! I have all kinds of issues."

Don't let Donny and Marie Osmond (the singing siblings from the 70s) fool you. Since the beginning of time, siblings have been waging war. If it wasn't Adam and Eve's sons, Cain and Abel, fighting over lambs and straw, it was Bobby and J.R. Ewing battling for oil and Ms. Ellie's love.

Sadly, our home was not immune to sibling rivalry. We were always waiting for the perfect opportunity to sabotage each other.

> *"My sister wears a bra!"* a young Gina would screech out the bedroom window for all the neighborhood boys to hear.
>
> *"Mom! Gina just clocked the girl across the street with a 7-iron!"* said a young Patty (the first to discover Gina's exceptional golf ability).

This rivalry occurs when one sibling feels the other is getting more attention. In most cases, it's for a positive achievement, like a good report card or a sporting accomplishment. But in many families with disabled children today, siblings are jealous for a whole different set of reasons.

> *"Come on, Mom! Pleeeeeeeeeease write about me! I have all kinds of issues."*
>
> *"How come she gets to have a learning disability. It's not fair!"*
>
> *"What! She got to ride in an ambulance? I want a seizure, too!"*
>
> *"I'm working on a book, too. It's called* Shut Up About Your 'Special' Kid!
>
> *"Mommy, how come she gets to eat the Ritalin candy? I want some."*
>
> *"Why does she get to go to a special school? Aren't I special, too?"*

The simple fact is when you're so worried about your special child, it's often hard to make your other children feel special. Of course, we've discovered that this can come back to haunt you.

An All-to-Familiar Ring

Parenting a bipolar child is a lot like having your entire family walking on a tightrope. Every move has the potential for dangerous vibrations that can cause the entire family to spiral downward.

So when your bipolar child is sad, you have to be very careful and quick to comfort them.

"Cheer up, Jennifer, Bo just wasn't meant to win American Idol.*"*

And when they're manic, you want to avoid anything that could set them off.

"Yes, I think that red tube top goes very well with your purple ski pants."

The only thing more difficult than keeping your bipolar child from plunging into a downward spiral is to keep your entire family from going with her, something we discovered on a recent family vacation when we took a nature hike in the mountains. As we stopped to take a break by a river, Jennifer accidentally dropped her new cell phone into the water.

She didn't share her news until we returned from our hike and had gone out for ice cream.

"Mom, I did something awful," she said with tears in her eyes.

"Oh, I know, but your older sister Jules had to find out about the Tooth Fairy sometime. She is 15, you know."

"No, Mom, I dropped my new cell phone in the water," she sobbed. *"I'm so sorry!"*

"It's OK, Jenn," I said, hugging her. *"It's only a phone. If it doesn't dry out on its own, we'll just get another one."*

"I'm so sorry!" she wailed. *"Will you ever forgive me?"*

As soon as Jennifer was out of earshot, her older sister stomped up to me with her ice-cream covered mouth gaped open.

"Like I don't like believe like what just happened?"

"Whatever do you mean?" I asked innocently.

"I mean like when I like left like my new cell phone (which by the way was your like old cell phone) like in my soccer bag and my water bottle like leaked and wrecked it, you like freaked saying that I was like 'irresponsible and immature.'"

"Well, that's different," I said trying to figure out what Shirley Partridge would have done in this situation had her family been dysfunctional.

"No like don't tell me, Mom, like it's like different because like Jennifer is like 'special' and she gets away with everything."

"You're right, Jules. I was wrong. So how about I buy you another ice cream?"

"Like cool. Can you make it like a double scoop?"

Search and Rescue 911

Patty

When our daughter, Jennifer, was in the midst of a devastating depression, it took its toll on the entire family, including our then 4-year-old son, Michael, who was feeling neglected *("Mommy, you never play with me anymore!").* To cheer him up, I planned an adventure to a strange and somewhat faraway place – my parents' house.

When we arrived, my father was unloading tomato plants from his car. In our customary Italian way, I gave him a big hug, kissed him on the cheek, and then went in to see my mother who was standing over the stove in her housecoat, stirring sauce. *"Hi Patty! Where's my adorable little grandson?"* she excitedly asked.

I looked behind me, but my son was nowhere to be found. Curious, I went downstairs and called, "*Michael James? Where are you?*" When I received no response (something I was quite used to with his father), I walked outside to see my father.

"*Hey Dad, is Mikey with you?*"

"No," he replied. *"I thought he was with you."*

"SAINT ANTHONY!!!" cried my mother who had crept up behind me. "Tragedy Magazine *just did a story about missing kids."*

Confident that he was somewhere on the premises, the three of us scoured the house calling for him. *"Mikey? Here Mikey."*

Again no answer.

After about 20 minutes, I got in my car to see if my little "Houdini" had wandered down to the nearby playground.

He was nowhere to be found.

When I spotted a police cruiser passing by, I casually rolled down my car window and said, *"Hmm. Excuse me, officer. My son is well sort of… misplaced."*

"Repeat," she commanded.

"It appears I misplaced my …"

Before I could finish, she flicked on her lights and got on her radio. *"Charlie, this is One-Nine. We have a MWF here who says her 4-year-old son is MIA. Code 30. Over."*

Having grown up with *CHiPs* and *Adam 12*, I quickly realized that she was not taking this matter lightly – a fact that was confirmed when three police cruisers and two fire engines showed up at my parents' door. Before I knew it, neighbors started showing up with baked goods, consoling my mother, *"Poor Vi, are you OK? I made you an upside down cake to cheer you up."* The gravity of the situation really hit me when the town's Council on Aging van pulled into the driveway. The senior world was now involved; this was getting serious!

When one of the officers asked my mother for my son's preschool picture and a piece of his clothing for the police canine, I was in full panic, picturing Mikey's adorable little face on a milk carton.

Then I heard one of the officers holler, "*We got him!*"

There, sitting on my parents' doorstep was my son, who had been found crouching between a couch and end table in the basement.

The officer turned to me and said, *"Here he is Mom! Your little guy is right here, nice and safe. Give him a big hug."*

Overcome with stress from my daughter and now my son, I shrieked, *"Hug?! I want this kid scared straight! Throw him in lock-up!"*

"Mommy, can you go to jail, too? We can snuggle together."

"SAINT ANTHONY!" cried my mother. *"Do you know how many germs there are in those cells?"*

Following "Teacher's" Instructions

With busy school and sports schedules, it's becoming increasingly difficult for my family to spend time together and communicate. And because our family dinner has become the only time when we can all sit down together, I've made the most of this time, lecturing my children about the importance of spreading goodness throughout the world.

"OK kids, what did you do to make the world better today? Jules would you like to go first?" I asked, turning to my oldest.

"Well like I like helped open the door for this like totally random girl even though she can sometimes like be a real like jerk."

"OK, Jules, that's not exactly what I had in mind, but thank you anyway."

"Michael, how about you?" I asked my 8-year-old son, hoping that I would have taught at least one of my children one of life's valuable lessons.

"Did you do anything today to make the world better? "

"As a matter of fact, I did, Mom," he proudly declared. *"Two kids in my class were fighting and the teacher asked my advice on how to handle it."*

"And what exactly did you tell her, Michael?" I asked, curious.

"Well Mom, I told her what you always tell Julie and me when Jennifer is acting out."

"And what's that?" I asked, feeling a sense of pride that perhaps I had mastered this motherhood thing.

"Well, I told her not to look at them or breathe near them."

Sister Act

Gina

One of the most amazing aspects of being a parent is watching your children do the things you did as a child. *("Don't worry, Katie, you didn't hurt my feelings. I used to make fun of my mother's hairdo, too.")* Of course, it's not always the good stuff. My two daughters are constantly fighting, reminding me of how much I couldn't stand my sister as a child. My younger daughter, Emily, for example, is always competing with her older sister, waiting for the opportunity to make Katie look bad to me.

Often, she'll use Katie's quirkier habits to score points with me and her father.

> *"Dad, Katie's flapping a pair of scissors!"*
>
> *"Mom, Katie's chewing on your hairbrush again!"*

Emily's jealousy toward Katie has even gotten to a point where I can't give Katie a compliment without sending Emily into a tailspin.

> *"You look so pretty today, Sweetie. Your eyes are so blue,"* I said to Katie to build her up.
>
> "*WAAHHHHHHHHH!*" cried Emily.
>
> *"What's wrong, Honey?"* I asked baffled.
>
> *"I'M UGLY! YOU THINK I'M UGLY!"*

And those rare occasions when Emily actually does something I ask of her presents another opportunity to make Katie look bad.

> *"Emily, thank you so much for setting the table! You're so sweet!"*
>
> *"And Katie's not sweet, right Mom, because she didn't help you?"*

When it comes to her little sister, Katie really isn't sweet. A big prankster, Katie often likes to make Emily and her playdates victims of her creative (and often diabolical) plans.

> *"Dad! Katie toilet-papered my room and told Annie she was adopted."*
>
> *"Mom! Katie put slime on top of my bedroom door!"*

I'm hoping this is just a phase. And that maybe one day, they will follow me and my much, much older and not-quite-as-smart sister's footsteps and stop looking for opportunities to make each other look bad.

Of course, we'd be lying if we said siblings fight all the time. Some (ours, of course, excluded) actually amaze their parents with how well they get along.

Danny's Little Girl

Since he was a baby, Danny, an 11-year-old with a non-verbal learning disability, has adored his 15-year-old sister, Jocelyn.

"Joce, I'm going to marry you someday."

"Mom! Dad! Tell him to stop saying that! He's creeping me out!"

One evening, Danny, his parents, his sister, and his sister's new boyfriend went out to dinner. As Danny watched his sister lovingly gaze into the eyes of her boyfriend, he turned to his parents and said, *"Mom, Dad, I'm losing her."*

Future "Survivor"

One day, while playing in his home, Quinn, a nature-loving boy with PDD, came upon a ladybug. He placed it on his hand and giggled as it tickled his skin.

"Look, Papa!" he proudly declared to his father. *"It's a ladybug!"*

"That's right, Quinn," said his father smiling.

Excited, he brought the bug to his baby sister.

"JoJo look!"

"Yay!" screeched JoJo, clapping her hands.

"Ummm ummm good!" said Quinn as he promptly placed the bug into his mouth and swallowed.

"Yay!" screeched JoJo again.

STeba

Chapter 11

CRAYOLA MINIVANS, HIGHWAY FLASHES, AND OTHER "NORMAL" EVERYDAY LIFE OCCURRENCES

"Sorry I missed the bus Mom, I was practicing my funny faces in the mirror."

In addition to warning us about the hazards of falling bathtubs at The Home Depot, and the hidden dangers of wax build-up on coffee tables, our mother constantly likes to give advice. In fact, in the course of a day, she dishes out more than Martha Stewart. And though the subjects of her ongoing lecture series vary, she is constantly telling us that we need to stop and smell the roses or in her case, the lemon fresh Pledge. "*Your lives are too busy. You need to slow down, enjoy your lives, and shine your kitchen cabinets.*"

We know she's right. But when you're juggling a husband, kids, house, career, and *American Idol,* it's pretty hard to do. It's a common theme among most parents, especially parents who have children with disabilities. That's because children with disabilities are often on their own schedules – schedules that generally aren't conducive to meeting a school bus in time or evacuating the house in a family fire drill.

> *"Katie! The bus is almost here! What are you doing in the bathroom so long?"*
>
> *"Oh, nothing. I was just practicing my funny faces in the mirror. I'm getting really good."*

As you can see, Katie seems to have no trouble stopping and smelling the roses. Maybe she's on to something.

That's Yesterday's News

Gina

When we moved into our house, my husband and I fell in love with the roomy closets and spacious wine rack. (*"Just think about all the Riunite we can store here."*) What we failed to notice was the winding driveway that required the use of a mountain goat to climb. The harsh reality of our driveway hit us when we received our first Sunday morning newspaper delivery.

Not wanting to scare away our new neighbors with my bedhead, I sent my daughter, Katie, to retrieve the paper. I kissed her at the doorway and watched her make her journey down the stairs. She walked down a few steps and then stopped to follow a bird.

Several minutes later, she continued down the front walk, pausing to spend precious time to catch up with a caterpillar. When she finally hit asphalt, she stopped again, picked up a piece of sidewalk chalk, and wrote, *"I Love Mom."* Touched, I went back inside and began cleaning the house. Much later, I was just about to file a missing persons report when I heard the doorbell ring.

I was relieved to see that it was my daughter. *"Here's your paper, Mom,"* she proudly declared.

"Thanks, Honey. But this is yesterday's news. Could you do me a favor and go back down and get today's paper. And by the way have you grown? You look so much taller to me."

Case Clothesed

When my brother and I were teenagers, we used to host parties while our parents were away for the weekend. And while we thought we were always careful to destroy any evidence that would indict us, our mother always knew right away.

"Welcome home Mom! We missed you!"

"All right, when was it Patricia?

"When was what?" I would innocently ask.

"The party. When was it?"

"Mom, honestly we don't know what you're taking about," I said, crossing my fingers behind my back.

"Ah ha!" she shouted in Felix Unger fashion. *"I knew it!"*

"How did you know?" we conceded.

"Because there were teenage finger marks on the coffee table!"

"Oh," I, the one responsible for that department, said.

"And the guest towels were used!"

"Really," I said, glaring at my brother who was in charge of that department.

Although I will never be the super sleuth that our mother is, I do like to think that I, too, can be perceptive. Those years of watching Nancy Drew and Lieutenant Colombo crack cases have helped me hone my own detective skills – skills that come in handy when it comes to determining when my bipolar child is manic.

"All right, Jennifer, what's wrong?"

"Nothing. Nothing's wrong."

"Then how do you explain the piles of clothes that are forming a conga line outside your room?"

"Oh that! I'm just looking for the blue tank top and green flip-flops. I HAVE TO HAVE MY BLUE TANK TOP AND GREEN FLIP-FLOPS!"

"I see," I reply, removing her calendar from the wall and placing it under her nose.

"Would you please state the month on which this calendar is open," I say.

"JANUARY," she says.

Ready for the knockout punch, I say, *"And can you tell me whether we wear flip-flops and tank tops in January in New England."*

"No, we don't," she says meekly.

"Aha!" I knew it! You're manic!"

Green with Innocence

One summer, Ken decided to surprise his wife, Susan, with a special home improvement project while she and their children were away visiting her sister.

"Welcome home, Honey!" he said, greeting her in the driveway.

"I have something I want to show you in the basement," he said taking his wife's hand and signaling the kids to follow.

When they reached the basement, Ken said, "*So what do you think Hon? Did I do good?*"

"*Oh, Honey, I love it. Look at those shelves. And I just love the rainbow walls. Thanks so much, Honey,*" she said, running up and hugging her husband.

Inspired by his mother's joyous reaction, the next day, their 5-year-old bipolar son, Max, wanted to surprise his Mom and Dad with a home improvement project of his own.

So he rounded up his two-year-old brother and asked, "*OK, Mikey, what do you think? Purple, Red, Green? Blue? Yellow? Or Orange?*"

"Geen," said Mikey.

Pleased with his little brother's choice, Max pried open a can of green paint and handed his little brother a brush.

Together, they painted the driver's side of the minivan and the garage doors bright green.

When a horrified Susan came out of the house, Max ran up to his mother and asked, *"So what do you think, Hon? Did I do good?"*

Grin and Bare It

One snowy Super Bowl Sunday, Jane and her 4-year-old autistic son, Michael, were traveling treacherous highway roads on the way home from Grandma's house. Anxious, Jane got in the fast lane and locked in on the road ahead *("Just get us home safely! Please God!").* Her focus was interrupted by the sound of Michael's car seat unbuckling. *"Dear God! Not now!"* she thought fearful of what her little "Houdini" was up to.

All at once, memories of the last unbuckling incident, when he jumped in the front seat and attempted to drive the car, came flashing back.

With one eye on the road, and the other on the rearview mirror, Jane watched in helpless horror as Michael began shedding his Tom Brady shirt, pants, and underwear. Naked, he climbed up on the ledge of the rear window, creating a spectacle for all drivers to see and leaving Jane with a difficult "Game Day" dilemma of her own.

> *"Do I make my move like a running back, cut to the outside, cross three lanes of traffic, and risk killing us both?"*

> *"Or, do I pass like Tom Brady, let him stay, and pray no one calls DSS on me?"*

She chose the latter, cranked up the heat, and made it home for the half-time show, which happily did not feature DSS.

A Big Waste of Time

It's not uncommon for children with special needs to have quirky habits and fixations. Aleck, a young boy with autism, was no exception as he became obsessed with cars, trucks, and more recently, plastic bank cards.

So when his babysitter, Paula, learned that her husband had arranged to have their septic system cleaned, she was ecstatic telling Aleck's mother, "*Wait until he sees that truck! He's gonna go crazy.*"

The entire week before, Paula worked Aleck in a frenzy telling him about the truck. *"Only two more days until the big truck comes, Aleck!"*

When the big day finally arrived, she rounded up the truck driver for a brief sidebar.

"Look, I have a little boy in there who just loves trucks. Can you kind of play it up big time? Show him the hose and everything."

The septic driver looked at her strangely and replied, "*Whatever, lady.*"

Moments later, an excited Paula brought Aleck into the driveway where the truck was parked.

"OK, Aleck! You can open your eyes now!" she shouted with excitement.

Frantic, Aleck flew past the septic truck, ran up to the driver, and breathlessly asked, "*Can I see your bank card? Can I, huh?*

Shut up
I have the tip

Chapter 12

NO MORE PENCILS, NO MORE BOOKS, NO MORE TEACHER'S DEPRESSING CALLS

"In her snowflake essay, your daughter just threatened to blow up the school."

Throughout our lives, we have learned simple principles we know to be true. The sun will rise in the East and set in the West. The earth will always rotate on its axis. And no matter how hard we clean our houses, our mother will always find a dust bunny *("Tell me when is the last time you girls dusted your ficus trees?").* But now that we're parents, we have stumbled across another truth – a simple one that really applies to parents of all children, including perfect ones:

No good can come from a school call.

Granted, in this modern era of technology, we at least have the benefit of advance warning. But not even that can take away the anxiety of seeing the school's name lit up on Caller ID like a Christmas tree. (It's worse than seeing your mortgage company name.)

Here are just a few examples of calls we and other parents have received over the years.

> *"It's the nurse. Your son just vomited his sloppy joe."*
>
> *"In her snowflake essay, your daughter threatened to blow up the school."*
>
> *"Mom, can you bring me my slippers? It's Pajama Day and I forgot them."*
>
> *"Your son is putting green Play-Doh up his nose. It's very distracting to the children."*
>
> *"Your child was chewing on the castanets in music class."*
>
> *"Mom, I think I forgot my Ritalin. I figured it out when I got sent to the principal's office."*
>
> *"Your second-grader is exhibiting gang-like activity."*
>
> *"I caught your 11-year old sniffing dry erase markers. I'm a bit concerned."*
>
> *"Mom, you got the days mixed up. Today is School Picture Day NOT Crazy Hair Day."*

And if you've ever tried to call a teacher back, you know that you have a better chance of connecting to the Oval Office. *("Mrs. Gallagher, I'll be available from 10:59 to 11:00 if you want to call me back.")*

Call Me Positive

For once, wouldn't it be great to receive calls for positive reasons? Calls like:

> *"Just wanted to tell you how smart your child is."*
>
> *"Your daughter is such an angel. You should really have more kids."*
>
> *"FYI, we just promoted your child to the next grade because he is gifted."*
>
> *"Thanks for being a good Mom and packing my straw hat for Farmer's Day."*
>
> *"This is the school nurse. I'm just calling to tell you how healthy your child looks. Keep up the good work."*

A New School of Thought

Faced with increased academic and social stress, young Elizabeth, a girl with autism, had a very difficult year during fifth grade. And not surprisingly, during that time, her mother, Carol, received frequent calls from the school telling her about the struggles Elizabeth was having. *("Yes, this is the principal. Elizabeth kicked a boy for teasing her.")* It got to the point that every time the phone rang, Carol was in full panic, waiting for them to tell her about some new problem.

And on those very rare occasions when the phone rang and it wasn't the school, she was giddy.

> *"Oh thank God, it's just you Citibank. Sure, I'll get that late payment in right away. Thanks so much for calling. Feel free to call back and yell at me at any time."*
>
> *"That's great that I won a prize and everything. But you can keep it. I'm just glad you're not my daughter's school calling with another problem."*

With sixth grade and those tender middle school years facing Elizabeth, Carol and her husband considered a smaller school environment. So with the help of a consultant, they enrolled Elizabeth in a new school with just a handful of students. With small class sizes and students with issues similar to Elizabeth's, Carol hoped that Elizabeth would get the individualized attention and understanding she needed.

Of course, she wasn't aware that that individualized attention would mean one very important thing – more school calls.

Elizabeth was not at the new school for more than a few days when Carol saw the school's name on Caller ID.

"NO! NOT AGAIN! IT CAN'T BE HAPPENING AGAIN!"

Fingers trembling, she prepared for the bad news that was sure to come.

"Hhhhhello," she answered.

"*Mrs. Martin. This is Nancy at the office. Nothing's wrong.*"

"*WWWWhat ddddid you say*?" Carol asked.

"Nothing's wrong." Nancy repeated.

"*Dddidd you just say nothing's wrong?"* she repeated. *"Wwwhy would you cccall if nnnothing is wwwwrong?"* she asked perplexed.

"Oh, I just wanted to see how Elizabeth was getting home today. She has Homework Club."

Shocked that a school would call for a non-negative reason, Carol gathered herself and responded. *"Oh, I'll be picking her up."*

"Great!" she said. "*Have a good day!*"

"*Wait!*" Carol said, using the opportunity to confirm what she had just heard. *"You're sure nothing's wrong?"*

"Nope, everything is just fine."

"You're sure?"

"Yes, I'm sure."

Since that day, Carol has received numerous calls for the school for various reasons (none of which have involved any problems). She's even learned to relax a bit, too.

"Hi GMAC Mortgage. Yeah, I'll get that mortgage payment right out. Now can we please get off the phone? My daughter's school might be trying to call to discuss the lunch menu."

❧ Oooh! Oooh! Pick Me Teacher! ❧

Parents don't just receive calls for the things their children do; sometimes it's simply for things their children say. Karen, mother of Ben, a boy with ADD, received an interesting call from the teacher one day.

Ben's class was studying the Internet.

> *"Class, what do we use the Internet for?"* his teacher asked.
>
> Ben shot his hand up like a stock market surge. *"I know, I know. Pick me!"*
>
> *"Yes, Benjamin,"* the teacher responded.
>
> *"We use the Internet to help us with homework and look up pornography."*

❧ Important Note for Teacher ❧

Preparing for an important school meeting about the concerns she was having over her 11-year-old son David's education, Lauren gathered valuable feedback from David.

> *"Now Honey, Mommy's going to talk to the teacher about some of the problems you're having in school. Is there anything you want me to tell her?"*
>
> A thoughtful child with ADHD, David scratched his chin and said, *"Oh, yeah there is one thing. When you're talking to her, can you kind of work into the conversation that…well… I hate her!"*

When No News Isn't Good News

To facilitate communication with teachers, some parents of special needs children use communication logs, or backpack notebooks that allow parents and teachers to send notes back and forth. Tina tried using one with her daughter, Samantha, but many times it came home blank because there was nothing to report. Eager to see how it worked, Tina sent in her first note.

"*Testing 1-2-3 testing.*"

When she didn't receive a response she wrote, "*Hello, hello, can anyone hear me?*"

Apparently, the teacher was not amused because the notebook could not be found in the backpack after that.

Chapter 13

BEING A PART OF THE SOCIAL SCENE

"I'll give you some bubblegum if you play with my daughter."

When we were foolish teenagers, we were afraid to be seen with our parents. We had a great system in place when it came to school dances.

"OK, Mom, you can drop us off here."

"But it's raining and the school is two miles away."

"Really Mom it's fine. We could use the exercise."

"OK, fine, but can I fix your hair before you get out of the car?"

Happily, we're over that stage of pretending not to know our parents. Our parents, on the other hand, seem to be giving it back to us in their golden years.

"So Mom, can you buy these pants for me with your senior discount?"

"All right, but if anyone asks, I don't know you. Now get lost!"

We didn't realize it when we were kids, but it really wasn't about our parents (OK, maybe a little). It was because we were frightened to death of standing out or being different. It's ironic that our children stand out on a daily basis either for the way they think, the way they look, or the way they act or express themselves. *("Mom, all the kids think I'm weird because I can't stop flapping my hands.")*

It's true for a lot of children with disabilities. We may realize it when we see them playing alone in the sandbox or camping out by the phone waiting for it to ring (we both know something about that from our dating days). The good news is that often our children are strong and resilient and probably don't know any other way. The bad news is that the worry alone can keep a parent up all night like a teenage girl slumber party.

No Contest

When we moved into our new neighborhood, our daughter, Katie, was eager to make friends. With Asperger's syndrome, and social difficulties, it was no easy task.

"How come none of the kids are coming over, Mom?" she asked, looking out at the boys and girls shooting baskets across the street.

"Let's see what Mommy can do," I said, already working out a plan in my head.

The next day, I put on my hightops and dribbled over to my neighbor's house with Katie, her little sister, and a bag of bubblegum in tow.

> *"Hey kids. Anyone want to play hoops?"* I said, blowing a bubble the size of Rhode Island.
>
> *"Woah! Yeah!"* said the oldest of the kids.

It was a brilliant and successful plan. Within weeks of moving in, I had them eating Dubble Bubbles out of my hands. And though my daughter quickly became friends with them, my plan was taking its toll on me, as kids would come to the house at all hours asking me to play with them. One Friday evening around 7 p.m., three of them knocked at my door, bouncing a basketball.

> *"Hey Gina,* (our "candy bond" put us on a first-name basis)*, do you want to have a contest?"* Lucas, the youngest of the three asked me, batting his big brown eyes.
>
> *"Look guys, I'm really tired. It's been a long week of work, and I just want to relax."*

He shrugged his shoulders and dribbled away signaling for the others to follow.

Moments later, the phone rang. It was my new neighborhood buddy, the mother of two of the children.

> *"What does she want? Don't tell me she's going to harass me about this!"* I thought.
>
> "*So why aren't you coming over 'Louise' (*my neighborhood nickname earned from our impromptu Friday afternoon happy hours*)*? *Do you have something more important to do?"* she asked, grilling me like a Burger King Whopper.
>
> "*Look 'Thelma,' I'm really tired. I had a very bad week of work, and I don't feel like running around in the driveway."*
>
> *"Who said anything about running around in the driveway?"* she asked, confused.
>
> *"Well the kids came over and said they wanted to have a contest, and I'm just too tired to compete."*
>
> "A *contest?"* she repeated, laughing. "*I told them to go over and invite you*

for a cocktail."

"Oh a cocktail? In that case Thelma, I'll be right over."

A Devil of a Question

Kids with Asperger's syndrome are often very gullible, taking people at their word. Katie is no exception as she demonstrated on her 11th birthday, when she came rushing into the house with tears streaming down her face.

"*What's wrong Honey?* I asked, impressed with my mother's intution.

"*Mom, I have a question, and I want the truth.*"

"*What is it, baby?*" I asked, going down to her level and looking into her bloodshot blue eyes.

"Am I the devil's child?

"Excuse me?"

"*The devil. Am I his child?*

"*Well, believe me, I'm the first to admit that your father is not perfect, but I can say with a high degree of certainty that he's not the devil. Where did you get that from?"*

"Well today is my birthday 6/6/06. And Jake said that makes me the devil's child."

"*Honey, he's just kidding you. Besides, your were born in 1995 not in 2006.*"

"So I'm not the devil's child?"

"No Honey, you're not. You have to be careful not to believe everything that people tell you."

"So when you keep telling me that the stork brought me. Are you telling the truth?"

"It's the truth, Honey. I swear."

Honk If You Love Jesus

Sleepovers. They're as much a part of American teen pop culture as MTV, loud music with nasty words, and shorts with words scrawled across the buttocks.

"Mom are my 'Buzz Off' shorts still in the laundry?"

And whether teens are guests or hosts of sleepovers, the end result is always the same: junk food and endless chatter that keeps them up well into the night. The next day, parents are rewarded with a grumpy teen who often responds to questions in one-word grunts and refuses to do anything but sleep.

However, if you're the parent of a bipolar kid, the nightmare can linger for days.

"Ummm, Jenn, do you think you could lie down somewhere else? I don't think the dog likes to be used as a pillow."

"Ugh! I'm so sick of you telling me what to do!"

It's not like my husband and I weren't warned. When we received Jennifer's bipolar diagnosis, the doctor was very clear.

"Bipolar children need their sleep. This is critical."

And for those first couple of years, we avoided sleepovers quite nicely. It wasn't until she turned 13 that we were faced with a difficult decision. We knew what the doctor told us, yet we wanted her to experience those annoying rituals of teenhood.

And so, I recently allowed my daughter to host a sleepover with three nice and polite friends. They slept in the basement, and I did not retire to bed until I knew they were fast asleep around 1 a.m.

As expected the next day, Jenn was like a grizzly bear with hangnails. I did my best to stay clear of her, and was successful until 5 p.m.

"OK guys. We're going to church. Get ready," I told my other two children.

"*Awww,*" they said. "*We were hoping you'd forget.*"

"*You have exactly five minutes to get ready.*" I said, synchronizing my watch.

"*And on your way up, please tell Jennifer to get ready,*" I said, cowardly avoiding dealing with the child who doesn't handle spontaneity – the kid who demands to know in advance when I am going to the mailbox.

When my other two children came down without Jenn, I did the unthinkable.

"*OK, kids, I'm going in!*" I said, heading up the stairs toward Jennifer's room.

"Be careful, Mom!" they warned.

When I walked into her room, she spun her head around like Linda Blair in *The Exorcist* and screeched, "*GET OUT*!!!"

"*Sure Jenn. No problem. We'll just wait for you in the car,"* I said, rushing out.

I could have sworn I heard her hiss as I left the room.

As Jules, Mikey, and I waited in the sanctity of my car, Jules made an astute observation.

"*Uh like Mom, I don't think like Jennifer like wants to like come with us.*"

"*What makes you say that, Jules*?" I asked.

"*Uh because she's throwing things out the window*," said my son.

Minutes later, Jennifer joined us, but not before she kicked the door and cursed at me.

Once we arrived in the church parking lot, Jennifer refused to get out of the car.

"*That's OK, Jenn,"* I said, eager to escape from her.

"*Just worship that crucifix on the dashboard and that will count,"* I said rushing the other two along into the church.

"*Not fair*!" said my son.

Not surprisingly, we arrived several minutes late, earning a spot in the vestibule with 60 of our fellow tardy parishioners.

Moments later, I heard a blaring car alarm. There were well over a hundred cars in the lot but I (and my other two children who looked up at me with bulging eyes) was painfully aware of where that sound was coming from. Very quietly, I lowered my praying hands into my pocketbook, while trying frantically to find the mute button on my keychain.

All around, my fellow parishioners were whispering, "*Oh that's so rude! Why doesn't that person shut off that car alarm*?"

After several minutes, Jules whispered, "*Mom like give me like the keys. I'll like go outside and like shut it off.*"

About three minutes later, Jules returned with my keys and whispered to me, "*Like Mom. That like brings new meaning to church bells.*"

An Appreciation for Teacher

When one of the boys in his class made a disparaging remark about his teacher, Andrew, a child with social issues, was devastated. "*That's not right. I have to tell Ms. Hancock,*" he thought.

After class, he marched up to the teacher and recounted the precise details (memory is one of his greatest strengths) of what his classmate said. "*And he said that you were so ugly you belong in the zoo...*"

The next morning, when the boy found out who ratted him out, he confronted Andrew. "*WHY DID YOU TELL ON ME? I'M GONNA KILL YOU!*"

All day long, Andrew walked the hallways petrified of what might happen to him.

When he got home from school, he confessed to his father, a tough, hard-working man's man who doesn't hold back.

"*Dad, there's this kid at school who wants to beat me up! He said something mean about the teacher and I just had to tell her!*"

"*ARE YOU CRAZY ANDREW? If I was that kid, I would beat you up, too! Why did you tell?*"

"*I had to, Dad. It wasn't right. I couldn't let him get away with that. It's Teacher Appreciation Week.*"

Up Against the Clock

Children with disabilities often want to be like everybody else and experience the same childhood rituals. Alison, a fifth grade student with dyslexia, was no exception. One day, when she got off the bus with tears in her eyes, her mother was very concerned.

"What's wrong, Honey?"

"It's awful, just awful. All the girls in my class have boyfriends. I want one, but none of the boys like me because they think I'm not smart."

"Now, now Honey, you're a little young yet. Someday when you're old enough, you'll meet a boy who loves you just for you."

"I can't wait forever, Mom. I'm already 10."

Tickled Pink

The president of a new and successful collections company, Bob, couldn't wait until his first company dinner when he would introduce his family to his employees and partners. His son, Daniel, with ADHD, wasn't as eager. *"Do we have to go, Dad? It's so boring!"*

The dinner was a success. Dessert, however, was a different story. As the coffee cups were being set down, Daniel got up on his chair and made a startling announcement:

"My Dad wears pink underwear!"

Laurel, Bob's crafty wife, used to doing damage control after her son's impulsive outbursts, quickly explained, *"Well, I did the laundry today and accidentally washed Bob's tiger print Fruit of the Loom boxers with my pink blouse. To make a long story short, it ended up making Bob's underwear pink."*

Not letting that ruin his moment, Daniel got up again, this time announcing, *"My Dad is losing his hair in chunks!"*

"Not sure I can do anything with that one Bob!" Laurel said throwing her hands in the air.

Chapter 14

TRUTH OR CONSEQUENCES?

"Mom, I can't clean my room! I have a learning difference and it's just too hard!"

Growing up, or parents had very strict rules – brush your teeth before bedtime, never wear white before Memorial Day, and always help with the dishes after a meal. One of us (who shall remain nameless) had a little difficulty with the last one. Often when it came to time to do the dishes, she would fake a headache and take off like a Boeing 747, leaving the "good sister" fuming, and standing up to her elbows in Dawn. Sadly, our naïve parents saw nothing wrong with the scenario, "*Leave her alone, Patty; the poor thing is sick.*"

For any parent, it's difficult to determine when their child is playing them and when they're telling the truth. But when you have a child with a disability the decision to discipline or not to discipline is more challenging than some of their homework assignments *("How am I supposed to remember what a polygon is?").* That's because there's a very fine line between what *they are* capable of and what *they say they are* capable of.

Earth to Mommy – You're Being Played

Gina

When you're a parent, you have to be able to step in and help your child when he or she is experiencing difficulties. That's especially true when it comes to school projects, which are always difficult for Katie given her motor difficulties.

Whenever Katie is assigned a project, I'm always by her side imparting my knowledge and support (*"I'd like to punch your teacher for assigning this!")* in hopes she will fly on her own someday. Sometimes my plan doesn't work out the way I expected as I learned on our last collaboration, a model of the solar system.

> "*Mom, this planet project is too hard,*" Katie sobbed while accidentally splitting a Styrofoam Pluto in half with a toothpick. *"I'm just no good with my hands."*
>
> *"I know, Honey,"* I said, wiping a tear from my bloodshot eyes. *"Mommy will finish it for you."*
>
> "*OK, Mommy, I think I'll go play Playstation with Dad to calm down.*"

The next morning when Katie and my husband, Mike, came down for breakfast, I was still sitting at the kitchen table fumbling to put a tennis bracelet around Uranus.

> *"How was your night, Honey?"* I asked Katie.
>
> *"Great Mom. I made it all the way to the top level and saved Bikini Bottom."*

"You should have seen her, Gene. She's amazing with her hands," my husband proudly declared.

An Allowance for Effort

Every Christmas, as our children tear through their endless supply of Christmas gifts *("A WNBA Barbie! Thanks Mom!")*, my parents like to tell my brother, sister, and I about their childhood holidays.

"Kids today have too much!" our father says with disgust, carefully salvaging bows and tape from the torn wrapping paper.

"Do you know what we got in our stocking when we were little?" asks our mother, holding open a used trash bag for him.

"Tangerines," my brother, sister, and I say in unison, painfully familiar with this story.

"Yeah, and they weren't even seedless," adds our father.

Because of my parents' humble citrus beginnings, it was very important that their three children grew up understanding the value of hard work and labor. So when we were little, they assigned each of us various chores in exchange for a small allowance.

"Gina, vacuum the shag rug!"

"Patty, dust off the plastic grapes!"

"Bob, go wash the Plymouth Fury!"

Grateful for the work ethic they instilled in me, I've attempted to institute this same policy with my special needs daughter, Katie. But given her difficulties managing everyday tasks, I have to carefully consider what type of work she should be compensated for. And I learned quickly not to ask for her feedback, since her idea of work differs vastly from mine.

"Katie, could you please dust the armoire?"

"What? You didn't pay me for the last thing I did!"

"What did you do?" I asked, mystified.

"Well, I got out of bed!"

"That's ridiculous!"

"Oh, and by the way, you didn't pay me for flushing the toilet, so you owe me for that, too."

Scout's Honor

With dyslexia and a hearing impairment, Mary, a girl with an extremely high IQ, was tired of being the subject of ridicule from her classmates.

"You can't spell. You're so stupid!"

One afternoon, after a difficult day of cruel teasing, Mary went to her Brownie meeting. As part of the end of the meeting ritual, Mary gathered in a circle with the other girls, held their hands, and recited the Brownie Pledge.

I will to my best to be,
Honest and fair,
Friendly and helpful,
Considerate and caring,
Courageous and strong, and
Responsible for what I say and do, and
Respect myself and others,
Respect authority,
Use resources wisely,
Make the world a better place, and
Be a sister to every Girl Scout.

As Mary was reciting the words from the bottom of her heart, she was crushing the hand and stomping on the foot of the little girl next to her, the ringleader of the mean girls at school.

When Mary's mom picked her up from the meeting she was eager to hear how it went.

"So how was the meeting, Mary? Did you have fun?"

"Oh yes, Mommy," smiled Mary sweetly, as she held up her hand for the traditional Brownie salute. *"Scout's honor."*

Snow Job

One day, when Gino grew tired of seeing his 12-year-old son, Mario, with ADD, playing video games, he made an important decision.

"We're going skiing!"

"But Dad! It's cold out!" whined Mario.

"It'll be great. You'll get fresh air and exercise."

That afternoon, Mario and Gino hit the slopes. As they were making a run down a small trail, Mario fell and yelled, *"My leg! My leg! I can't move it! It's broken!"*

Knowing his son had a flair for the dramatic, Gino was just about ready to tell him to "suck it up" when he was interrupted by the flashing lights of the Ski Patrol. Before he knew it, Gino was watching three men fussing over his son.

They gingerly placed Mario on a sled and brought him down the mountain.

"You doing OK, Little Guy?" asked one of the patrolmen.

"Hang in there, Buddy!" said another, stroking Mario's forehead.

When they reached the parking lot, they lifted Mario off the stretcher and handed him over to Gino.

Gino shook their hands and said, *"Thanks, I can take it from there."*

"Are you sure?" asked one of the men. *"The poor kid. He's in rough shape!"*

"He sure is," said another, wiping a tear from his eye.

"Don't worry! I'll take good care of him," replied Gino with confidence.

As the patrolmen walked away, Gino gently put his son down. When they were finally out of sight, he turned to his son and asked, *"You ready, Mario?"*

"Oh yeah," Mario said, taking off in a full sprint toward the car.

"Good, cause I'm gonna kill you!" yelled Gino chasing after him.

"Special" Benefits

Special needs children are not the only ones who use their disabilities to their advantage; their parents are often guilty of playing "the special needs card" to get what they want. It worked for Paula, mother of Mary, a 6-year-old girl with PDD, when one of her new neighbors came over to complain about Paula's new swingset, which was located a mere two inches over the neighbor's property line.

> *"Your swingset is on my property!"* the neighbor snapped. *"I'd like it moved by tomorrow at the latest."*
>
> *"Oh we're so sorry. It seemed like the perfect place for our little girl, Mary. She has special needs you know. It's the only thing that makes her smile these days. But don't worry, we'll move it."*
>
> "*Oh, never mind! Leave it!*" the neighbor said, wiping tears from her eyes. *"Just leave it!"*

By Daniel

Chapter 15

FINAL THOUGHTS FROM "MARCIA" AND "JAN"

"When are we going to be rich, Mom? I want my swimming pool."
"Yeah, and I want the maid you promised me!"

Though she would never admit it, our mother was a huge fan of Carol Brady, the perky mother on the '70s sitcom *The Brady Bunch*. We're not sure if it was Carol's trim figure that won her over, or the fact that she had Alice, the maid, do all the cooking and cleaning. Whatever the reason, it was painfully obvious that our mother adored her (her copycat beehive hairdo pretty much said it all).

And like her hero often did, our mother would ask us what lesson we learned on those rare occasions when one of us committed a wrongdoing. It's a parenting ploy she still uses on us today, especially when she comes to visit.

> *"And what did we learn, Patty?"* she asks, while handling a tarnished brass lamp.
>
> *"I learned to Never, Ever use Windex on brass."*
>
> *"Good girl. Now give mother a hug. And remember not to play ball in the house."*

In the spirit of our mother and Mrs. Brady, we thought it would be fitting to rap up this exciting episode in our lives and share the lessons we learned in the process of writing this book. And boy did we learn a lot (and not just that writer's block is a disability in and of itself).

The Only Label that Matters

When we conceived the idea for this book, our first thought was about our daughters. How would they feel about sharing their personal stories and labels with the world? Would we make their already difficult lives more difficult? We weren't sure, so we asked them. And just as they've done so many times in their young lives, they amazed us with their insights.

Katie's View

For most of her life, Katie has been a kid who likes to fly under the radar.

> *"Mom! The teacher brought in the newspaper column you wrote and showed it to the kids. Can you please stop writing that thing? It's so embarrassing. Everyone was staring at me."*

So when I asked her about the possibility of writing this book and sharing her Asperger's diagnosis with the world, her answer surprised me.

"So what do you think, Katie? Can I write this book about you?"

"Sure. Great. Maybe we can get rich off my learning difference and get me a swimming pool."

"Are you sure? Everyone is going to know that you have Asperger's syndrome."

"Yeah, so. Who cares?"

Jennifer's View

Like Katie, Jennifer warmed to the idea. Well, at least at first.

"Yeah, it's a great idea. Maybe it will help a kid with bipolar disorder feel better."

As time passed, however, Jennifer's interest waned. "*That's all you talk about is that book.*" And unlike her brother and sister, she no longer asked me to read aloud what I had worked on that day.

"Mom! Like read us what you wrote today!" pleaded my older daughter, Jules.

"*Yeah, Mom!*" said my son.

"I'm going upstairs!" said Jenn.

Although this was not totally unexpected from a child in middle school, where a single pimple can be social suicide, I was disappointed, particularly since Jenn had always been so open about being bipolar with her friends.

It got to a point where my sister and I had to have a serious discussion about the future of the book.

"SAINT ANTHONY!" said my sister, sounding like our mother. "*We can't go forward with this book without her blessing. We could ruin her life and make things worse. I think we should stop. Remember her sticky notes.*"

"Let's give it awhile," I said, not ready to give up on my daughter.

About a week into the new school year, I was sitting at my kitchen table pondering how we could do the book without Jennifer. My thoughts were interrupted when Jennifer flew through the door and handed me a piece of paper.

"Mom, can you help me with this?'

"OK, Jenn but if it's math homework, you know my cutoff is third grade. Once they start combining the alphabet with numbers, I'm lost," I warned.

"Don't worry, Mom. It's not algebra," she said giving me the sweet smile I've always cherished.

As I looked at the paper, I saw that it was titled "The Person Whom I Most Admire." I had assumed it was about me and my tremendous parenting skills and how I *(sometimes)* manage to get the right kid to the right field at the right time and still provide dinner *("OK kids, do you want Chinese takeout or pizza?").*

To my surprise, it was an essay about my sister. It's not that I was surprised that she wrote about my sister. Gina did after all have some good qualities – humor, basketball skills, nice earlobes. But it was why she chose my sister that surprised me. She wrote:

> *"My aunt is tall, humorous, and always has a positive attitude toward life. She and my mom are in the process of writing a book. It is about kids with different kinds of disabilities and uses humor to let people feel that they are not alone in this world. I thought it was very thoughtful of my aunt and my mom to take the time to create a fabulous book that makes kids with learning differences and illnesses feel more comfortable. After reading the book that my mom and my aunt had put such tremendous effort in, it made me want to contribute to it."*

I immediately called my sister and told her the news. Not surprisingly, she was ecstatic (though not for the reason I expected).

"Uh, huh, she wrote about me. Uh, huh! I'm her hero. Woohoo! Who's the best aunt?"

Jennifer's review of the book was the most important and best we'll receive. The fact that she and Katie were willing to share their "labels" with the world at such difficult times in their lives was pretty amazing and not at all surprising. After all, these two little girls have shown their courage their entire lives.

And as we talked to other parents and learned about the courage and resiliency of other children with a range of special needs (autism, bipolar, dyslexia, PDD, cerebal palsy, etc.), we realized that only one label really applies for ALL these kids - "heroes."

Dreams Can Come True – Maybe Even Weight Loss Ones

Over the years, we've both shared a love of humor. Just ask any of our poor friends and relatives who get flooded with our joke emails and crank calls on a daily basis *("Don't you two have jobs?")*. We've both dreamed about channeling our humor into a book someday, but never imagined it would be for such a worthwhile cause. We also never fathomed having so many mothers and fathers rally behind us *("You guys are going to be famous!")*. Even our family members, who once were a bit skeptical *("Sure, you're going to write a book and I'm the Queen of England")* have changed their tune and are now on board ("sipping the Kool Aid").

> *"Can I tell you both something? You girls need to get your nails done before you meet Oprah. They look horrible,"* said our mother.
>
> *"Now don't go giving away free copies to people,"* said our father.
>
> *"Can we hire a maid yet?"* asked Gina's husband, Mike.
>
> *"No Mommy! I don't want to read any more books,"* said Gina's daughter, Emily.
>
> *"What are you writing again, Patty?"* asked Patty's husband, Michael.
>
> *"Whoa! Like that's like so sick dude!"* exclaimed Patty's daughter, Jules.
>
> *"Mommy, can you pay me back my First Communion money now?"* said Patty's son, Michael.

This book is proof that dreams really can come true, and it's a powerful lesson for our children. And though our "other" dream to lose weight and drop two sizes hasn't come true yet (we've both been on diets since 1978), we're not giving up yet.

Gina's Final Lesson

By now, it's probably pretty clear that my daughter, Katie, and I are complete opposites. When I was young, I would have been classified as a perfect kid, though my sister has a slightly different opinion. *"You perfect? Yeah, right."*

But the truth is, I excelled at everything I did. I was always the first kid picked for sports *("We got Gina. Na! Na! Na! Na! Na!")*, one of the top students in the class *("You got another 'A'!)*, and the person kids always wanted to be around *("I called it first. I'm sitting with Gina!")*. As an overachiever, I was always focused on my next goal, never once stopping to enjoy the ones I achieved along the way.

I was also paralyzed with a fear of failure. If something got hard, I wanted to quit.

"Dad, the basketball coach yelled at me today! I'm quitting!"

"Mom, I don't want to take advanced classes. They may be too hard!"

In contrast, throughout her entire life, my daughter Katie has struggled at nearly everything she does – playing sports, making grades, finding friends. It was enough to leave me, a classic overachiever, chronic worrier, and lifetime pessimist, awake night after night pondering the same burning question: *"How will she develop her self-esteem?"*

But what I failed to notice that despite all her difficulties, socially, academically, and athletically, my daughter is happier and more self-confident than I ever was. She's taught me to appreciate the little accomplishments in life – things that most people never stop to appreciate.

"Dad! Guess what? I answered a question right today at school!"

"You'll never believe this Mom! I got invited to a birthday party!"

" I told a joke and all the kids laughed."

"Dad, I did a jump on the skateboard. This is the best day of my life!"

And when things get tough, she bounces back like a superball.

"The kids on the bus all made fun of me today because I flap my hands."

"Well it's settled then. I'm driving you to school."

"No way Mom! I love to ride the bus. If I don't go on the bus, then that's letting them win."

Even more amazing is that despite all her struggles, she has never given up on herself or lowered her expectations.

"I can't decide if I want to be a singer or a veterinarian."

"Honey, I think you should be a veterinarian because I've got to be honest, you can't carry a tune in your backpack."

"But Mom, you can be anything you want to be if you put your mind to it."

Before I began writing this book, I wanted to find a miracle cure for Katie's Asperger's *("I'm serious Mike, let's take her to Lourdes or Medjugorje!")*. But through this magical process, I realized it's just as much a part of her as her beautiful blue eyes or sun streaked hair. To cure Katie of her Asperger's would take away the innocence, the pureness, and even the quirkiness that I love most about her.

> No, I no longer want to change her; I want to change the world by helping them see what Katie has helped me see – and that's the incredible beauty and individuality of Katie and "imperfect" kids like her.

Yes, it's hard to believe that this lifetime pessimist no longer sees Katie's glass as half-empty, but overflowing with possibilities. I no longer think about what she *won't* become, but what she *will* become. I don't dwell on what she *can't* do, but the amazing things she *can* do.

I invested a great deal of time, energy, and money into this book; I never expected such a tremendous return that will pay me dividends for the rest of my life.

Patty's Final Lesson

They say the first born is generally the most intelligent and successful in a family. This, however, was hardly the case in my family. I was a good student – not a great one. I was a good athlete – not a star one. In fact, I never excelled at anything except for one thing – being average. Often, I would tell people, *"I like being average. It comes with no pressure."* And unlike my little sister and brother, I was never the type to set goals; I was pretty content to go with whatever life threw my way.

Jennifer's illness was no exception. At first, I was in denial, refusing to believe that my daughter would lead anything other than a normal life. But over the years through all our trials and tribulations, hospitalizations and medications, and through support from other parents in similar situations, I've realized that Jennifer has made me better – a fact that Jennifer doesn't even realize to this day.

> *"Mom, why would you want to write about me?"* she asked me one evening before going to bed. *"I feel like all I ever did was disrupt this family."*

With a lump in my throat and tears in my eyes, I told her the gifts she has given me:

> *"Jennifer, because of you, I am a better person.*

Because of you, I'm not as materialistic as I once was.

Because of you, I've learned to take each day one at a time.

Because of you, I no longer sweat the small stuff.

Because of you, I'm not so quick to judge people.

Because of you, I've learned to have a deeper appreciation for family.

Because of you, I have met some truly wonderful people whom I never would have met.

Yes, Jennifer, because of you I am better and the world is better."

What's even more rewarding is that despite their constant fights, Jennifer has made her older sister a better person, too. Her sister summed it up best when she said, *"Mom, it's like this thing with Jennifer is so bad that like sometimes I don't want to come home. But you know what Mom? I see kids at school like trying to act cool and worrying about like what guy they're going to date. We're the lucky ones."*

Our experience with Jennifer has made my son a better person, too. At age 8, he received a school recognition award for helping a girl in his class with Down syndrome with her math homework.

Some may pity my daughter and my family. To those folks, I say this is a gift – a gift of wisdom. It's our job to share it with the world.

The "Real" Beauty of this Book

When we decided to write this book, we had dreams of building fame and fortune and impressive credentials for our next high school reunions *("So what if we gained a few pounds, we'll wow them with our new book.")*. But as we met mothers and fathers of special children, we learned that the process of writing a book was about so much more than that.

On this amazing journey, we've talked with parents whose children may never walk, talk, or ever live with them at home. These parents have missed out on little events and milestones that so many of us take for granted – listening to their child read or say "I love you," watching their child ride a bike for the first time, or even tucking their children in each night. Yet what's most remarkable is that these special people manage to persevere, and handle whatever life throws at them and their child with humor, grace, and poise.

Yes, even in our perfection-crazed world, we found warm, wonderful people who had the courage to be real. Mothers and fathers willing to openly discuss their greatest fears, joys, hopes, failures, and weaknesses, and who despite their challenges and pain, have the strength and compassion to offer hope and comfort to others, including complete strangers.

Our dear friend, Jane Lynn, a retired teacher, counselor, and psychiatric nurse who was with us throughout the entire process, put it best after observing one of our Saturday night focus group sessions with married couples.

> *"Think about it! It was a Saturday night and here were 5-6 families sitting around talking NOT about their latest golf score or cruise ship experience or desire to become wealthy BUT about their FAMILIES!!! IMAGINE THAT!!! People who sincerely wanted to change themselves, their children's experience of the world, their own experience because they knew there must be a better way. And it was a Saturday night! They could have partied a million places but they all chose to be a part of this process in Gina's family room."*

We couldn't have summed it up better ourselves. And while we can't take credit for her profound thoughts, we can take credit for taking such a wise, thoughtful friend on this journey with us.

The Greatest Story of All (And It Doesn't Even Include a Disney Character)

We both know that raising a child with a disability affects not just the child, but the entire family as well. But we sometimes forget that family goes beyond our own dinner tables. Grandparents are deeply affected too, and most especially our mother. If you haven't noticed, she's a chronic worrier *("SAINT ANTHONY!")*, who has had sleepless nights worrying about our daughters and the impact their struggles have had on us.

> *"Gina, you look so tired. What's wrong?"*
>
> *"Nothing's wrong. Everything's fine."*
>
> *"You don't look fine; I worry about you and your sister so much."*

At times, her love and concern makes it so easy for us to break down and become her little girls all over again, especially Gina, her highly sensitive child.

> *"I'm just so tired of the worrying Mom. Why Mom? Why? Why does Katie have to struggle so much? It's not fair!"* Gina said, sobbing.
>
> *"I know. I know. I pray for her every day,"* she said, hugging her with the same arms that got us both through so many of our own childhood struggles.

For our mother, family and religion are everything. So it's not at all surprising that she often turns to God to see her family through difficult times (though we sometimes question her methods).

> *"Patty, put this St. Dymphna pin in your bra close to your heart. She's the Saint of Mental Illness."*
>
> *"OK, Ma, but please let me do it myself."*

Our love for her and hers for us is why she's been such an integral part of this book process, sometimes even more than she wanted *("Are you girls writing about me again? People are going to think I'm a nut!")*.

She's shared our excitement *("I really love the book girls. I'm so proud of you both!")* and watched us, particularly, Gina, who shares her anxiety, transform right in front of her *("I'm not sad anymore, Mom. I now realize what a blessing Katie's Asperger's is.")*.

And just as we've learned from our daughters, she's learned from us.

We didn't realize it until she approached us one day and said, *"You know girls, I don't worry about Katie and Jennifer anymore."*

"You don't?" Patty asked, shocked that the woman who stayed up at night worrying about bathtubs falling on us at The Home Depot or having her grandchildren sucked up in hotel swimming pool drains, would be so calm about the kids she loved so much.

"No, they're going to be fine. I don't even pray for their disabilities to go away any more."

"Really Mom? No more calling the prayer hotline?"

"Nope."

"No more St. Dymphna in your bra?"

"Nope."

"No more rosary beads on the clothesline?"

"Well, that has nothing to do with the girls. That's about the weather."

"Wow, Mom. That's great!" we both said, giving her a bear hug, and realizing she never felt so soft and comfortable.

"Yeah, and you know what else girls?" she asked, stroking our hair.

"What?" we asked, waiting for her to tell us to grow our nails or scrub the grout in our bathrooms.

"Now that I think of it, I really like your hair. It's so…so…what's the word I'm looking for? It's so…"

"…Imperfect!" we say in unison, smiling at each other.

"Yes! That's it! Imperfect!"

And that our dear readers, is the greatest story of all.

IMPERFECT GLOSSARY

ADD (attention deficit disorder)
A condition, usually in children, marked by inattentiveness, dreaminess, and passivity.

ADHD (attention deficit hyperactivity disorder)
A condition, usually in children, characterized by inattention, hyperactivity, and impulsiveness.

Asperger's Syndrome
A psychiatric disorder, most often noted during the early school years, characterized by impairments in social interaction and repetitive behavior patterns.

Autism
A psychiatric disorder of childhood characterized by marked deficits in communication and social interaction, preoccupation with fantasy, language impairment, and abnormal behavior, such as repetitive acts and excessive attachment to certain objects.

Bipolar Disorder
An affective disorder, previously known as manic depression, characterized by periods of mania alternating with periods of depression, usually interspersed with relatively long intervals of normal moods.

Cerebral Palsy
A form of paralysis believed to be caused by a prenatal brain defect or by brain injury during birth, most marked in certain motor areas and characterized by difficulty in control of the voluntary muscles.

Down Syndrome
A lifelong condition in which a person is born with distinct physical features, such as a flat face and short neck, and some degree of cognitive disability. Although Down syndrome is permanent, most people who have it are able to live healthy, productive lives.

Depression
A condition of general emotional dejection, withdrawal and sadness greater and more prolonged than that warranted by any objective reason.

Dyslexia
A learning disorder marked by impaired ability to recognize and comprehend written words.

Mitochondrial Defect
A disease that results from failures of the mitochondria specialized compartment present in every cell of the body except red blood cells.

Non-Verbal Learning Disability
A neurophysical disorder originating in the right hemisphere of the brain, which results with problems with visual-spatial, intuitive, organizational, evaluative, and holistic processing functions.

PDD (pervasive developmental disorder)
Any of several disorders, such as autism and Asperger's syndrome, characterized by severe deficits in many areas of development, including social interaction and communication, or by the presence of repetitive, stereotyped behaviors. Such disorders are usually evident in the first years of life.

Ritalin
A central nervous system stimulant used in the treatment of narcolepsy in adults and in the treatment of attention deficit disorder (ADD) in children.

WISC (Wechsler Intelligence Scale for Children)
An intelligence test for children of elementary- and secondary-school age that tests knowledge and abilities of a verbal nature (as vocabulary, comprehension, and verbal mathematical reasoning) and the application of knowledge and various skills to the performance of specified tasks (as the arrangement of a series of pictures into a meaningful sequence and the assembly of an object given its parts).

Sources include dictionary.com, WebMD

About the Authors (and Their Mother)

Though they couldn't stand each other as young children growing up in Maynard, Mass., Patricia and Gina Terrasi have developed a wonderful bond of mutual respect, support, and bad hair days.

Patricia, the sister afraid of success, is the mother of three children – Julianne, Jennifer, and Michael – and resides in Andover, Mass., with her husband Michael. She owns Champion Video Productions, which offers world-class, professional sports recruitment videos and award-winning event videography.

Gina, the sister afraid of failure, is mother to daughters, Katie and Emily, and resides in Marlborough, Mass., with her supportive and patient husband Michael, *("I have to do laundry again!")*. Gina is a Hatch award-winning copywriter who provides writing and strategic consulting services to several of New England's leading businesses.

Despite the constant ribbing she put up with in this book, their mother, Viola, is very proud of her daughters for writing the book. *"I love both my daughters. I don't play favorites. I fix both their hair."*

Acknowledgements

They say the most wonderful part of reaching a goal is not the goal itself, but the journey. This was certainly true in the course of writing this book.

Along this life-changing adventure, we have crossed paths with caring, intelligent people who have raised our consciousness and made us better mothers, people, writers, and businesswomen. And at the risk of sounding like Academy Award recipients (minus, of course, the expensive dresses and pretty hair), we'd like to now take the opportunity to thank them and give them shameless plugs.

First to our parents, Vi and Tony Terrasi, for creating a supportive, loving environment where siblings do not compete, but revel in each other's accomplishments and treasure their time together. This collaboration is a testament to your success as parents.

To our supportive husbands, Mike and Michael, who have put up with us over the past few months *("Don't you have any idea how hard it is to write? If you don't be quiet, we'll write* Shut Up About Your Imperfect Husband!"*).* Your love is unconditional, and we are truly blessed to share our lives with you.

To the rest of our clan – our children Julianne, Michael, and Emmy, and dogs, Rocky and Max – who have had to take a backseat to this project *("Please write about us. We're not perfect either.").* And to our supportive brother, Bob, and his beautiful children, Jess and Daniel, (who provided illustrations for this book). We're proud of you and hope you will see that dreams really can come true.

To our "second" sister, Laurel, we love you always.

To Vera for your encouragement and constant support throughout this journey. And for teaching Patty the importance of discipline with a special child.

To the late Katherine "Kay" Gallagher. Your spirit and sense of humor lives on through your granddaughter, Katie.

To our intelligent, passionate, and loving cousin Joanne Stropparo who embodies all the selfless qualities of motherhood.

To our talented cousins, Donna Saia, for illustrating the "Shut Up" parrot and world-class Executive Chef, Steve LaCount (*www.chiarabistro.com*), for believing in us.

To Mary and Nanci who shared our joy and excitement and told the entire senior population of the state of Florida about our book. To all our other wonderful aunts and uncles, Marion, Honey, and Ann who have laughed at our jokes over the years *("You two are full of hell!")*. To Auntie Jean, one of our biggest supporters, who never doubted for a second that we would write this book.

To our close friends and neighbors – Jules "Thelma," Polly, Cindy, "Bubbles," Christine (our beloved blogger), Ellen, Chuck, Kathy, Jeff, Paula, Tara, Dawn, Carol, and Kathleen – who shared our excitement and helped us spread the Movement of "Imperfection." And to Bob G. who withstood some tough peer pressure from the guys at work *("What the heck are those stupid bumper stickers on your truck?")*.

To the amazing moms and dads who supported us with their stories – Cheryl and Tony *(the greatest storyteller in the world)*, Ursula and Jim, Karen, Mary, Kevin and Meghan (author of that great line *"Why wasn't there a lifeguard at our gene pool?")*, Laurie, Karen, Prisca, and all the West Newbury moms who helped make this book possible. Meeting you has been one of the greatest treasures of having a "special" child.

To Mary, a special kid, who shared her triumphs to inspire others.

To Rhonda Taft-Farrell for seeing the potential of Katie and other special children.

To Dr. Leslie Spieth, Dr. Deirdre Logan, and Sally McCue, LICSW for your words of encouragement and beautiful letters that will adorn the walls in the future home office of Shut Up Industries, Inc.

To Jackie MacMullan, our favorite sportswriter, who provided invaluable guidance and support.

To the team of business professionals with whom we had the privilege of working, most especially, our "Chief Bad Ass," Bob Gottlieb, who helped us make all those tough business decisions *("Should we name the book "Shut Up" or "Be Quiet?")*.

To out talented creative team, Michael Surabian and Neil Grossman of Asagio Media (asagiomedia.com), who worked on our website and book design, and who put up with our endless changes. To Peter Fallon and Paul Walsh of The Creative Source (thecreativesource.net) who designed our awesome logo.

To Sharon Verbeten, our editor, and new mother of her beautiful "imperfect" newborn daughter, Holland. Meeting you was truly a blessing.

To June Clark, who believed in us and our message from the beginning.

To Ellen Murphy of Top Cat Promotions (*www.topcatpromotions.com*) who tolerated our constant barrage of promotional ideas (*"Why can't we have a talking Elmo that says, Shut Up?"*).

To Deb DiSandro (*www.slightlyoff.com*) who provided invaluable advice and guidance. To Julia Fox Garrison (*www.juliafoxgarrison.com*) for sharing your publishing experience with us novice authors. And to V. John Alexandrov, best-selling author (*www.moneychi.com*), who believed in us and shared the secret to achieving your dreams.

To our brilliant legal team, Annette Hines (*www.hinescounsel.com*) and Gwenn Roos (*www.onsidecounsel.com*). We so enjoyed working with you and hearing women of your intelligence repeatedly saying "Shut Up!"

Lastly, we would like to thank the amazing Jane Lynn, our dear friend, neighbor, and advisor. Through your wisdom and guidance, you helped Gina turn one of the most difficult times in her life into the most wonderful with this book. We have treasured the time we've spent with you and all the contributions you have made including your wonderful line, *"Bipolar, by Golly!"* which helped get it all started. You have made us better writers, mothers, and people. It has been a privilege to spend time with you.

That's it! We're done! At the risk of being politically incorrect, God Bless you all!

Housekeeping Items
(not the kind our mother likes of course)

Additional copies:
To order additional copies of this book for your friends, family members, and other perfect and imperfect people in your life, visit www.shutupaboutyourperfectkid.com.

Bulk sale discounts are available. Contact info@shutupabout.com.

Speaking appearances:
To inquire about hiring Patty, Gina, (and their mother) for your event, email info@shutupabout.com.

Story/illustration submissions:
To submit stories about you and your amazing "imperfect" child for our website and future editions of *Shut Up About Your Perfect Kid!*, visit www.shutupaboutyourperfectkid.com.

To be a part of the Movement of "Imperfection" and order Shut Up merchandise, including statement-making t-shirts and car magnets, visit www.shutupaboutyourperfectkid.com.

General questions/comments:
Email: info@shutupabout.com
Or write: Shut Up Industries, Inc.
P.O. Box 673
Maynard, MA 01754

Can't Shut Up?
For your daily dose of happy medicine without the scary side effects, check out our "Shut Up About…" Blog at www.shutupaboutyourperfectkid.com.